H

Health Economics of Depression

This series has been supported by an educational grant from SmithKline Beecham Pharmaceuticals

PERSPECTIVES IN PSYCHIATRY VOLUME 4

Health Economics of Depression

Edited by

B. Jönsson
Stockholm School of Economics, Sweden

and

J. Rosenbaum
Massachusetts General Hospital, Massachusetts, USA

JOHN WILEY & SONS

Chichester · New York · Brisbane · Toronto · Singapore

Other Wiley Editorial Offices

John Wiley & Sons, Inc., 605 Third Avenue,
New York, NY 10158-0012, USA

Jacaranda Wiley Ltd. G.P.O. Box 859, Brisbane,
Queensland 4001, Australia

John Wiley & Sons (Canada) Ltd, 22 Worcester Road,
Rexdale, Ontario M9W 1L1, Canada

John Wiley & Sons (SEA) Pte Ltd, 37 Jalan Pemimpin # 05-04,
Block B, Union Industrial Building, Singapore 2057

Library of Congress Cataloging-in-Publication Data

Health economics of depression / edited by B. Jonsson and J.
    Rosenbaum.
        p.   cm. — (Perspectives in psychiatry ; v. 4)
    Includes bibliographical references and index.
    ISBN 0 471 93746 0
    1. Depression, Mental—Economic aspects.   2. Depression, Mental—
Treatment—Economic aspects.   I. Jönsson, B., 1944–
II. Rosenbaum, J., 1947–   .   III. Series: Perspectives in
psychiatry ((Chichester, England) ; v. 4.
    RC537.H43   1993
    338.4'33622'5—dc20   93-8864
                                                                              CIP

British Library Cataloguing in Publication Data

A catalogue record for this book is
available from the British Library

ISBN 0 471 93746 0

Typeset in Garamond 10/12pt by Inforum, Rowlands Castle, Hants
Printed in Great Britain by Biddles Ltd, Guildford

Contents

Contributors

P. Bebbington
MRC Social and Community Unit, Institute of Psychiatry, De Crespigny Park, London, SE5 8AF, UK

P. Bech
Frederiksborg General Hospital, Psychiatric Institute, Dyrehavevaj 48, DK-3400 Hillerod, Denmark

W.F. Boyer
Feighner Research Institute, 15725 Pomerado Road, Suite 206, Poway, CA 92064, USA

M.J. Buxton
Health Economics Research Group, Brunel University, Uxbridge, Middlesex, UB8 3PH, UK

P. Carlsson
Centre for Medical Technology Assessment, Linköping University, S-581 81 Linköping, Sweden

D.J. Currie
Human Psychopharmacology Research Unit, University of Surrey, Milford Hospital, Godalming GU7 1UF, UK

G.C. Dunbar
SmithKline Beecham Pharmaceuticals, 48–49 London Road, Reigate, Surrey RH2 9YF, UK

D.B. Fairweather
Human Psychopharmacology Research Unit, University of Surrey, Milford Hospital, Godalming GU7 1UF, UK

J.P. Feighner
Feighner Research Institute, 15725 Pomerado Road, Suite 206, Poway, CA 92064, USA

I. Hindmarch
Human Psychopharmacology Research Unit, University of Surrey, Milford Hospital, Godalming GU7 1UF, UK

B. Jönsson
Stockholm School of Economics, Box 6501, S-11383 Stockholm, Sweden

J.S. McCombs
University of Southern California, School of Pharmacy, 1985 Zonal Avenue, Los Angeles, CA 90033, USA

T.G. McGuire   *Boston University, Department of Economics, 270 Bay State Road, Boston, Massachusetts 02215, USA*

M.B. Nichol   *University of Southern California, School of Pharmacy, 1985 Zonal Avenue, Los Angeles, CA 90033, USA*

J. Rosenbaum   *Clinical Psychopharmacology Unit, Massachusetts General Hospital, 15 Parkman Street—WACC 815, Boston, MA02114, USA*

W. Rutz   *Department of Psychiatry, S-621 23 Visby, Sweden*

M.J. Stoker   *SmithKline Beecham Pharmaceuticals, 47–49 London Road, Reigate, Surrey RH2 9YF, UK*

J. Wålinder   *Department of Psychiatry, University Hospital, S-58185 Linkoping, Sweden*

B.A. Weisbrod   *Center for Urban Affairs and Policy Research, North Western University, 2040 Sheridan Road, Evanston, IL 60208, USA*

Preface

Cost-containment policies in many countries are forcing doctors to consider the cost of treatment as well as its clinical efficacy and safety. The mental health services are no exception to this, despite the special problems of measuring mental health status and the social costs of mental illnesses. This book introduces the concept of health economics and highlights its importance to the practising psychiatrist as well as to the health care manager. It is written by an international multidisciplinary faculty of psychiatrists, health economists, physicians and pharmacists. Different aspects of the economics of mental health are discussed and cost–benefit studies of programmes aimed at reducing the burden of mental illnesses, particularly depression, are presented. Clinically relevant economic evaluations are an important aid to good clinical decision making. Health economists and clinicians must work closely together to ensure that resources are used to the best effect for patients and the population at large. It is our hope that this book will contribute to this development.

B. Jönsson
J.F. Rosenbaum

1

Health economics in the 1990s

M.J. Buxton

Introduction

Health economics, and particularly the economic evaluation of health care technologies and medical therapies, has moved from being a topic of mainly academic interest to economists to an issue that has a key position on the agenda for the 1990s of a number of different groups of participants in health care. The language of cost-effectiveness is beginning to pervade the debate about choices in health care. What is more, choices are now becoming quite overt and are correctly beginning to be exposed to the glare of public and media attention, rather than decisions being taken behind closed doors or choices being made implicitly.

The underlying reason for the interest in health economics—the need to use scarce health care resources to maximum benefit for patients—is not new. Scarcity and choice have existed in the health care sector for years, and they will coexist for the foreseeable future. The situation is exacerbated by the existence or prospect of new technologies. Specific and dramatic technological advances in a number of treatment areas, such as organ transplantation or gene therapy, frequently catch the headlines and highlight vividly the extent of what is technically achievable *if* the resources are available. More generally a steady incremental flow of therapeutic improvements (particularly developments of pharmaceutical therapies) increases the potentially achievable health care benefits, but at a cost.

Thus the inevitable reality is that the resources available for health care are not enough to match the medical and scientific communities' combined capabilities to provide possible ways of marginally increasing the health or well-being

Health Economics of Depression. Edited by B. Jönsson and J. Rosenbaum
© 1993 John Wiley & Sons Ltd.

of society. In the UK the phenomenon was evident almost as soon as the National Health Service (NHS) had been set up under the misguided expectation that cost would fall once a backlog of illness had been treated. By 1953, after the NHS had been in existence for just five years, it was necessary to set up an official committee to enquire into the cost of the NHS and 'to advise how, in view of the burdens on the Exchequer, a rising charge upon it can be avoided while providing for the maintenance of an adequate Service' (Guillebaud, 1956).

Nor is the problem one that is unique to the UK and the NHS. All countries, however rich, and however their health care systems are funded, face the problem that the costs of what is technically possible and potentially beneficial for patients exceed the resources available. In the Netherlands, a government committee set up to examine how to put limits on new medical technologies and how to deal with rationing caused by scarcity of care concluded that 'choices in health care are unavoidable and necessary' (Dunning, 1992). In health care, as in any other sector of life, scarcity of resources makes choices inevitable.

Whilst none of these problems are new for the 1990s, what has changed dramatically is the context and environment in which clinical decisions are made. For many years the traditional health economists' model, with its emphasis on societal benefit and societal cost, has been seen as being at odds with the traditional clinical decision model emphasizing individual benefit irrespective of the cost of the resources devoted to the care of that individual. But two interrelated factors have changed: the perspectives of those involved in health care decision-making, and the budgetary and incentives structures in which they operate. This chapter explores these changes and attempts to draw from them implications for clinicians and for health economics.

The traditional clinical decision model

The traditional clinical decision model is summarized in Figure 1. It can be characterized as that of the individual doctor acting within the broad limits of what might be seen as professionally accepted practice, even if that practice has not been explicitly defined or evaluated. In this traditional model, the clinician made decisions with respect to the treatment of his patient on the basis of trying to do anything that might possibly benefit his patient. Costs were seen as irrelevant in pursuit of the best interests of the individual patient facing the doctor, particularly if a third-party payer, rather than the patient or doctor, had to meet those costs. There was always an undoubtedly worthy aim of attempting to maximize an individual's health (although the maximand of survival, irrespective of quality of life, may perhaps have served as an inadequate substitute). This individual ethic tended to be informed little by the patient's views but reflected implicitly the clinician's own value set. Not only should any treatment that might reasonably be expected to do some good be provided, but there was a technological imperative to be seen to try even if there was no real prospect of patient benefit. Professor Cochrane likened this sort of behaviour to a quote from T.S. Eliot (Cochrane, 1972). He suggested that his colleagues often acted:

> Not for the good that it will do
> But that nothing may be left undone
> On the margins of the impossible

More recently, the belief, that a technological imperative exists, and is undesirable, has been restated by Wennberg (1990) who believes that:

> the current rates of use of invasive, high-technology medicine could well be higher than patients want . . . based on the hypothesis that, particularly when risks must be taken to reduce symptoms or improve quality of life, patients tend to be more adverse to risks than physicians. (p. 1203)

Empirical evidence on the attitudes and values of doctors is limited but studies do support the contention that physicians have a tendency to intervene (e.g. Ayanian and Berwick, 1991), that they have rather different attitudes to risk than their patients (e.g. McNeil *et al.*, 1982) and that they may value health states rather differently (Rosser and Kind, 1978; Kind *et al.*, 1982).

The traditional health economics model

Economists have traditionally argued from what is, for the most part, a completely different paradigm based on a collective, rather than individual, ethic

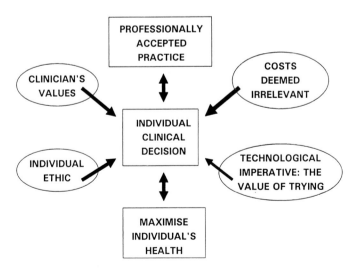

Figure 1.   The traditional clinical decision model.

and focusing on the relationship between costs to society as a whole and the benefits to society as a whole. The theoretical base lies in welfare economics, and its early applications to health care drew on applied models of cost–benefit analysis developed in the USA to address issues of large-scale state investment in such projects as multiple-purpose river developments (Sugden and Williams, 1978). Such developments had widespread implications imposing various costs on, and providing equally various benefits to, different groups, some directly and others only very indirectly affected by the projects.

In principle, the economist's maximand is societal well-being, within which health is but one factor. A number of studies, particularly of health care programmes in developing countries, have thus used changes in national product as a familiar, if very imperfect, measure of societal welfare. More commonly in developed countries, where the aims of the health care systems cannot reasonably be assumed to be to increase economic output, the value of health gain has often been the substituted simplification of the objective, and this has had the tendency to focus solely on outcomes, with the process of care being seen as having no inherent value. Thus the traditional health economics model can be characterised as in Figure 2.

Health care planning

The broad social perspective of the economist's model was an influence in some health care decisions, but mainly decisions were made at a system-planning or regulatory level. These clearly affected the resources available to

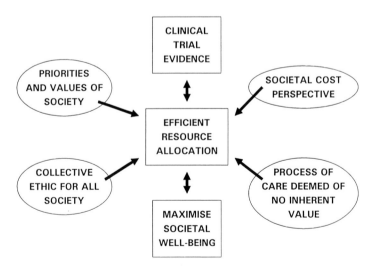

Figure 2.   The traditional health economics model.

doctors for individual patients, but nevertheless were sufficiently divorced from specific doctor/patient interactions for the disparities between the economist's and clinician's paradigms to remain implicit, and for the two models not to be seen as being in open conflict with each other.

Thus typically economic evaluation contributed to decisions about the provision of services, or location of facilities, or diffusion of new technologies. These decisions constrained at a macro level the resources available to the doctor, but did not directly impinge on the choices doctors make with regard to individual patients.

Thus economic evaluation has clearly been influential in the UK in decisions about screening programmes, from the early study justifying the cessation of mass radiography for tuberculosis (Pole, 1971) to recent debate on testing for high cholesterol (Standing Medical Advisory Committee, 1990). Similarly economic evaluation has been a key consideration in the diffusion of a number of expensive, and politically visible, technologies. For example, commissioned economic studies have played important roles in central decisions about the funding of heart transplantation in the UK, USA and the Netherlands (Evans *et al.*, 1984; Buxton *et al.*, 1985; Hout *et al.*, 1993).

Changing attitudes

But as the interest in cost-effectiveness has become more pervasive, and as it has begun to be related to clinical choices for individual patients, the differences between the two models have become overt, and some medical hostility has become explicit. In 1980, the *New England Journal of Medicine* published a letter reflecting this hostility:

> Of late an increasing number of papers in this and other journals have been concerned with 'cost-effectiveness' of diagnostic and therapeutic procedures. Inherent in these articles is the view that choices will be predicated not only on the basis of strictly clinical considerations but also on economic considerations as they may affect the patient, the hospital and society. It is my contention that such considerations are not germane to ethical medical practice . . . A physician who changes his or her way of practising medicine because of cost rather than purely medical considerations has indeed embarked on the 'slippery slope' of compromised ethics and waffled priorities. (Loewy, 1980, p. 697).

Whilst this view may be a particularly extreme position, denying as it does the relevance of cost considerations *even* as they effect the individual patient concerned, there is no doubt that many doctors would have shared the view that the cost implications as far as they affected some anonymous third party payer were at best irrelevant and at worst an unethical consideration.

But the divorcing of the value of a medical act from the cost of the resources it uses is not a tenable position. Nor is it a sufficient argument to contest that economic considerations impinge on clinical freedom. Jennett (1988), in supporting the role of economic evaluation, has deplored the way that under the guise of ethics:

> These 'clinical freedom fighters' hope thereby to legitimise their attempts to secure all possible services for *their* patients, regardless of the expectations of benefit relative to the prospects of other patients . . . (p. 28)

More generally there is a growing view from within the medical profession that practitioners in their dealings with individual patients have to take account of social responsibilities:

> For physicians and patients to retain the autonomy intrinsic to their professional relationship, social responsibilities must be incorporated into clinical decisions. Almost all clinicians would agree that, at some point, the extra money spent for tiny improvements in clinical outcomes is not worthwhile and represents inappropriate practice. The money thus misspent could have been devoted to medical care that would achieve greater benefit, or to some other meaningful social purpose. (Eisenberg, 1989, p. 2879)

This of course makes the whole process of determining appropriate care for individual patients a much more complex process, involving the balance of interests:

> Patients' interests must be weighed against the legitimate competing claims of other patients, of payers, of society as a whole and sometimes even of the physician himself. Although there is still a 'physician–patient relationship', it is now set within a broader health care nexus. In this context, the rights and interests of economic agents, society and other parties are both routine and proper, not exceptional or *per se* morally distasteful. (Morreim, 1991, p. 2)

This need to balance the interests of the individual and society arises in particular from the fact that in few health care systems do individuals pay directly from their own pocket for the bulk of the health care they receive. Instead elaborate systems of private insurance, public financing or indeed charitable provision of health care involve systems of individuals paying into a pool, according to a variety of formulae, and individuals—the same ones or others—drawing on that pool when the need arises. As Eddy (1991) describes the situation:

> Medicine has a long tradition of trying to maximize care for individual patients, a tradition not only based on compassion, but strongly reinforced by medical education, pressure from patients, families, the press, the

courts and professional incentives. But the act of pooling resources across individuals requires that the tradition be modified. In return for gaining the benefits derived from sharing costs, individuals must also accept some responsibilities and limitations. A responsibility is to respect others who contribute to the pool. A limitation is to not withdraw from it an unfair share. (p. 2406)

It is to the broader question of what constitutes a 'fair' share that economic evaluation must in future focus. The focus of economics is of course efficiency, with the proposition that to perpetuate an inefficient allocation of resources is unethical because it means that greater benefits for patients are being foregone than are being achieved by the existing (inefficient) use of scarce resources. But this position does ignore the questions about the equity of the distribution of care that may be consistent with an efficient distribution.

The changing economic environment

The factors that Eddy identifies as encouraging the traditional individualistic perspective are powerful and some will change only slowly. The popular media frequently jump to defend the rights of individuals who they claim have been denied expensive treatment for reasons of its cost, without stopping to consider the likely value of that treatment, the probability of its success, or the alternative uses to which the scarce resources might be put.

But, as indicated, medical thinking and education are beginning to change. And these changes are mirrored in, and to some extent hastened by, changes to the economic environment within which clinical decision-making takes place. World-wide, health care systems are undergoing reform. The organization, structure and incentive systems of health care systems are changing, and an underlying characteristic is that more and more clinicians are being given a clear responsibility for maximizing the value of the health care provided to a defined group of patients from a predetermined clinical budget. The precise form of these changes to the decision-making environment and the exact nature of the incentives differ between health care systems, but they contain elements of three key features.

The first such feature is that systems where fee-for-service has been the standard method of reimbursement are tending to move towards fixed prospective payments for particular categories of patients or conditions. In the USA, the introduction of payments by diagnostic related groups (DRGs) represents a far-reaching move towards a system of predetermined payment per episode of care. The effects of this are still rippling through the system and some of these effects have been analysed and reported (e.g. Kane and Manoukian, 1989). Many other countries have been exploring similar systems (Bardsley *et al.*,

1989). The common characteristic of these changes is that they place the onus on decision-makers to allocate resources so as to make the best use of a pre-determined fixed sum in providing care, either for a particular patient or for a group of patients.

The second feature is that increasingly it is *doctors* who are being given this responsibility. This is not an entirely new responsibility: doctors have always had to make decisions as to how to allocate their own time between their patients. Few would claim that a totally individualistic view determines that allocation. Any busy practising doctor has had to balance the likelihood that the particular patient currently in front of him might benefit from a longer consultation, or a more thorough examination or explanation, against the benefit of giving that time to other patients in the waiting room, the outpatients department or later on his ward round. Triage systems are accepted ways of determining the best allocation of available resources between competing claimants in real war, or in the battlefield of an overstretched accident and emergency department. But the new environment extends the clinicians' responsibility to make decisions concerning a broader package of resources used in the care of their patients. In the UK hospital sector, for example, relevant developments predate the current reforms. The Resource Management Initiative (RMI) was moving towards a system where clinical directors, usually clinicians, held relatively broadly based budgets to cover the costs of care provided to patients within their specialty or sub-specialty (Chantler, 1989). Early evaluation of the approach has suggested examples of doctors adjusting the combinations of resources to try to improve the cost-effectiveness of the care they provided (Packwood *et al.*, 1991). In many senses the voluntary acceptance of a broader responsibility, encouraged by RMI, has been overtaken by the new system of contracting between health care purchasers and health care providers. This is rapidly requiring that the system adopt clear prospective definitions of specialty-based, or even more precisely specified, workloads to be undertaken within a fixed contract at an agreed contract value or cost. Within their budget, determined by the contract, clinical directors then have to balance the best interests of the specific patient with the interests of the patients as a whole covered by the contract. Increased competition between providers for these contracts is seen as the means of ensuring that the best possible standards are achieved within the constraints of the budgeted resource level. Hospital doctors are thus given incentives to allocate resources cost-effectively within these clinically focused budgets in the manner that they believe will be to the best advantage of the patient group as a whole. Thus, for example, they will increasingly have the right incentives to adopt the use of a new and more expensive pharmaceutical product if they see from economic evaluation studies that it offers advantages to the patient and a net reduction in costs, through reduced hospitalization or nursing requirements (e.g. Khawaja *et al.*, 1989; Buxton *et al.*, 1991).

Similar changes are affecting primary care in the UK. General practices, which volunteer to become 'fundholding', are given budgets for their patients which cover not only services provided directly by the general practice but also pharmaceuticals prescribed, and some of the costs of secondary care in hospital. Such general practitioners now have every incentive to consider which combination of resources will provide the most cost-effective package of care for their patients, including some decisions about the balance of primary and secondary care. The early evidence is that fundholders are beginning to respond to these incentives and to consider ways of using health care resources more efficiently, or substituting alternative form, or locations, of care (Glennerster *et al.*, 1992).

The even more recent reforms for care in the community similarly shift professionals towards a position where they take greater responsibility for trying to provide the most appropriate packages of care for patients within predetermined budgetary limits (Henwood, 1992).

The third key element which features in the reforms of health care in various countries is an increasing emphasis on audit, on review systems and defined protocols (Pollitt, forthcoming). In part this is a reflection of a much broader change in public attitude towards professionals, and a growing reluctance simply to accept as an act of faith they always act in the best interests of their patients. In part it is a recognition by the medical profession that medicine today is too complex and the information base for clinical decisions too demanding for individual clinicians to make good decisions without carefully constructed decision aids and statements of standard approved practice. This view is of course reinforced by the understandable desire of individual clinicians to try to protect themselves from litigation by behaving according to externally validated 'rules'. But, whatever the reasons, such reviews and protocols can form an appropriate mechanism to incorporate proper consideration of the expected costs and benefits of particular clinical actions.

Of course such changes alone cannot ensure that cost-effective decisions are made, but each does provide an environment of more appropriate incentives. The net result is that many clinicians are now working within the framework, characterized as Figure 3, of the clinical resource management model.

The future

Enthusiasm for the general characteristics of these changes to incentives for efficiency should not be taken as endorsement of every detail or of a belief that they represent a panacea, guaranteeing a future in which each clinician makes consistently cost-effective decisions without problem or conflict.

One problem is that the boundaries of these clinically focused budgets are inevitably artificial, yet it will become increasingly difficult to persuade clinicians to take note of cost implications outside their own budgets. This is always true of systems with constrained budgetary responsibility: not worrying

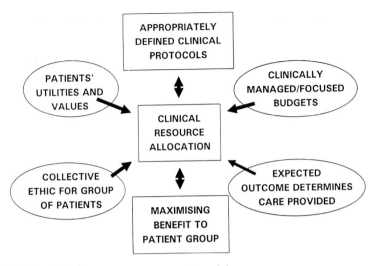

Figure 3.   The clinical resource management model.

about someone else's budget is behaviour we instantly recognize from within any large system. Where budgets have not been rigid, and constraints not too tight, then unselfish behaviour contributing to a wider good may well have been common. But once budgets become tight and pressures for greater 'efficiency' are increased, then such generosity is more difficult to sustain. In the past the NHS, in common no doubt with many other health care systems, has relied heavily on goodwill and altruistic, responsible behaviour. Whatever efficiency there was, existed despite the incentives built into the system rather than because of them. (For example, given the way in which hospital doctors have been rewarded and promoted in the UK, it is amazing that so much routine patient care has been undertaken.) But, as the rules of the game are drawn explicitly to achieve greater cost-effectiveness, rather than hoping that cost-effectiveness will be seen as a moral obligation by health care providers, then the more those providers are likely to play the game strictly according to the limitations of the rules, to work the system as best they can, and to leave it to the 'rule-makers' to cope with the anomalies.

Morreim (1991), adopting Jennett's guerilla warfare analogy, asserts that:

> when a physician 'games the system' in order to avoid, change, or undermine the system by extracting extra health benefits for his patients or himself he is quietly engaging in a form of revolutionary disobedience. (p. 86)

Whilst such a standpoint may strictly be justified, there must be a balancing onus on the 'rule-makers' to ensure that behaviour that follows the rules of engagement in the battle for resources is as consistent as possible with behaviour that is most likely to achieve the desired outcome.

But the changes will certainly provide an environment in which clinicians are increasingly interested in the economics of their detailed practice. Clinical managers competing for patients in general practice, or for contracts in secondary care, will become actively interested in economic evaluations of, for example, how alternative diagnostic sequences will affect costs and benefits, or how alternative drug therapies affect the total costs of hospitalization, or how screening programmes can be delivered most cost-effectively (e.g. Sculpher *et al.*, 1992). In evaluating drug therapies it will increasingly be necessary for health economics to go beyond simple head-to-head comparisons of single products to the evaluation of more complex therapeutic strategies, contrasting the effects of using different primary and secondary therapies, alternative selection criteria, and alternative rules for ending therapy.

In meeting these needs, health economics can usefully build on and integrate economic considerations into the growing body of literature using a decision tree framework to analyse the expected outcomes from medical decisions. If considerations of cost and patient utilities are incorporated into such models they can provide an excellent conceptual framework for developing and agreeing justifiable clinical protocols. Economists must meet the challenge of making their evaluations more relevant to the new decision context, of ensuring that their analyses are more transparent to users, and of working more closely with clinicians as they strive to improve the cost-effectiveness of their practice whether it be in the primary, secondary or tertiary sector, and whether it be capital-intensive high-technology medicine or low-technology time-intensive therapy.

Finally, in a collaborative quest for greater cost-effectiveness we must not ignore questions of equity. Economists must work with clinicians, patients, the general public (and their political representatives) to illuminate much more clearly the distributional implications of specific policies and generalized decision rules designed to maximize efficiency. The debate about the use of quality-adjusted life years (or QALYs) in relation to cost as a broad brush allocation criterion by health care purchasers is but one example of the issues that need much more discussion and some degree of social consensus (Buxton, 1992). We need to explore and make explicit the equity constraints within which society wishes health care to be provided.

Conclusions

Clinicians are increasingly accepting a broader social responsibility as allocators of scarce health care resources, which are typically paid for by complex pooling arrangements. In doing so they recognize that costs represent claims on resources that consequently have to be denied to other patients, and hence to consider the expected resource costs of proposed treatments in relation to the expected benefits for the patient is not an undesirable imposition but an ethical imperative. In so doing changing attitudes and incentives are leading clinicians to take key roles in clinical resource management.

If they are to take this responsibility seriously they need more, relevant economic information, appropriately framed to recognize the requirements, constraints and opportunities that the clinical resource management model provides. This implies that in the 1990s economists must collaborate with clinicians, from all specialties, to help them to better allocate inevitably scarce resources between the ever-increasing range of potentially beneficial health care interventions so as to provide patients collectively with the maximum possible health benefit. If not, clinicians *and* economists will be failing to meet their responsibilities.

Acknowledgement
Many of the ideas and some of the material presented in this Chapter have been developed and expanded, with permission, from an earlier paper given at a conference organised by the Office of Health Economics, in London, in 1989.

References

Ayanian AZ and Berwick DM (1991) Do physicians have a bias towards action: a classic study revisited. *Med Decis Making* **11**, 154–158.
Bardsley M, Coles J and Jenkins L (eds) (1989) *DRGs and Health Care,* 2nd edn, King Edward's Hospital Fund for London, London.
Buxton, MJ (1992) Are we satisfied with QALYs? What are the conceptual and empirical uncertainties and what must we do to make them more generally useful? In: Hopkins A (ed) *Measures of the Quality of Life and the Uses to which Such Measures May be Put*, pp. 41–49. London: Royal College of Physicians.
Buxton, MJ, Acheson R, Caine N, Gibson S and O'Brien BJ (1985) *Costs and Benefits of the Heart Transplant Programmes at Harefield and Papworth Hospitals*. DHSS Report No. 12. London: HMSO.
Buxton MJ, Dubois DJ, Turner RR *et al.* (1991) Cost implications of alternative treatments for AIDS patients with cryptococcal meningitis: comparison of fluconazole and amphotericin B-based therapies. *J Infect* **23**, 17–31.
Chantler C (1989) How to do it: be a manager. *Br. Med. J* **298**, 1505–1508.
Cochrane AL (1972) *Effectiveness and Efficiency: Random Reflections on Health Services.* London: Nuffield Provincial Hospitals Trust.
Dunning AJ (Chairman) (1992) *Choices in Health Care: Report of the Government Committee.* Rijswijk, the Netherlands: Ministry of Welfare, Health and Cultural Affairs.
Eddy DM (1991) The individual vs society: resolving the conflict. *JAMA* **265**, 2399–2406.
Eisenberg JM (1989) Clinical economics: a guide to the economic analysis of clinical practice. *JAMA,* **262**, 2879–2886.
Evans R, Manninen DL, Overcast TD, *et al.* (1984) *National Heart Transplantation Study,* Seattle, WA: Battelle Human Affairs Research Centers.
Glennerster H, Mastaganis M and Owens P (1992) *A Foothold for Fundholding*. Research Report 12. London: King's Fund Institute.

Guillebaud CW (Chairman) (1956) *Report of the Committee of Enquiry into the Cost of the National Health Service.* Cmd. 9663. London: HMSO.

Henwood M (1992) *Through a Glass Darkly. Community Care and Elderly People.* Research Report 14. London: King's Fund Institute.

Hout B van, Bonsel G, Habbema D, Maas P van der and Charro F de (1993) Heart transplantation in the Netherlands: cost effects and scenarios. *J Health Econom,* **12**, 73–93.

Jennett B (1988) Appropriate high technology: a painless prescription. In: Bunns TB and Firn M (eds) *Health Care Provision under Financial Constraint,* pp. 27–35. International Congress and Symposium Series No 115. London: Royal Society of Medicine.

Kane NM and Manoukian DP (1989) The effect of the Medicare prospective payment system on the adoption of new technology. *N Eng J Med* **321**, 1378–1383.

Khawaja HT, O'Brien BJ, Buxton MJ and Weaver PC (1989) Cost minimisation study of transdermal glyceryl trinitrate in reducing failures of peripheral intravenous infusion. *Br Med J* **299**, 97.

Kind P, Rosser R and Williams A (1982) Valuation of quality of life: some psychometric evidence. In: Jones-Lee M (ed.) *The Value of Life and Safety,* pp. 159–170. Amsterdam: North-Holland.

Loewy EH (1980) Cost should not be a factor in medical care. *N Engl J Med,* **302**, 697.

McNeil BJ, Pauker SG, Sox HC and Tversky A (1982) On the elicitation of preferences for alternatives. *N Engl J Med* **306**, 1259–1262.

Morreim EH (1991) *Balancing Act: The New Medical Ethics of Medicine's.* Dordrecht: Kluwer.

Packwood T, Keen J and Buxton M (1991) *Hospitals in Transition.* Milton Keynes: Open University Press.

Pole JD (1971) Mass radiography: a cost–benefit approach. In: McLachlan G (ed.) *Problems and Progress in Medical Care: Essays on Current Research,* pp. 47–55. Fifth Series, Nuffield Provincial Hospitals Trust. London: Oxford University Press.

Pollitt C (1993) The politics of medical quality: auditing doctors in the UK and USA. *Health Serv Manage Res,* **6**, 24–34.

Rosser R and Kind P (1978) A scale of valuations of states of illness: is there a social consensus? *Int J Epidemiol* **7**, 347–358.

Sculpher MJ, Buxton MJ, Ferguson BA, Spiegelhalter DJ and Kirby AJ (1992) Screening for diabetic retinopathy: a relative cost-effectiveness analysis of alternative modalities and strategies. *Health Econ* **1**, 39–51.

Standing Medical Advisory Committee (1990) *Blood Cholesterol Testing: The Cost-Effectiveness of Opportunistic Cholesterol Testing.* Report to the Secretary of State for Health. London: Department of Health.

Sugden R and Williams A (1978) *The Principles of Practical Cost–Benefit Analysis.* Oxford: Oxford University Press.

Wennberg JE (1990) Outcomes research, cost containment and the fear of health care rationing. *N Engl J Med* **323**, 1202–1204.

2

Economics of mental illness: costs, benefits and incentives*

Burton A. Weisbrod

Introduction

The post-World War II era has witnessed dramatic changes in health care throughout the industrialized world. Never in history have there been such enormous advances in knowledge and technology for treating the sick, such expansion of public and private systems for financing the utilization of that knowledge, and such explosive growth of health care costs. The percentage of national output going into health care has been growing in every industrialized country for decades. In the USA, for example, health care now constitutes 13% of the gross national product (GNP).

Health care costs are soaring largely because medical research and development (R&D) has generated an amazing arsenal of new technologies, which have been very costly. This is no mere coincidence. Financial incentives are the cause. Financial signals have been sent—through the health care finance system—to firms engaged in R&D, encouraging them to develop new diagnostic and treatment methods, regardless of cost. Society got exactly what was predicted: enormous technological advances but unprecedented increases in costs. (These ideas are developed at length in Weisbrod, 1991.)

Developing new technologies is one matter; using them is another. Traditionally, it has been physicians who decided whether any particular technology

---

* Paper presented at the 18th CINP in Nice, France. The health economics of depression: the cost of disease and the cost-effectiveness of treatment. 27 June 1992.

Health Economics of Depression. Edited by B. Jönsson and J. Rosenbaum

is 'worth' using. The cost of utilizing the technology, however, typically has fallen upon the larger health care finance system. Yet no system can long endure in which one party determines what will be done while another system finances those decisions. Thus, increasingly, physicians have found themselves in the difficult position of 'double agents'; historically, as agents for their patients' health care, but, in the post-World War II period, also becoming fiscal agents for private insurers and government. No one, however, can serve two 'masters'. The dilemma for public policy is how to gain the advantages of technological advances while containing health care costs. The dilemma for physicians is to determine the appropriateness of using new medical technologies while third parties—neither physicians nor their patients—are bearing the costs.

Efficient use of resources for treating the mentally ill

The incentives facing physicians and the medical R&D sector, the effects of health care finance mechanisms on those incentives, and the problem of cost containment are not fundamentally different in mental health than in other areas. Mental illness is diagnosed and treated with varied resources including physicians, computed tomography (CT) scanners and pharmaceuticals. Issues of cost-effectiveness, however, take some different forms in the mental illness area.

A major assumption that lies behind much of today's public policy towards health and mental health care is that individuals who are ill will seek help. Thus systems are developed to make medical resources available. Some mentally ill persons, however, do not voluntarily seek treatment. Sometimes it is inability to pay; sometimes it is lack of awareness of the problem or unwillingness to deal with it. The assumption that seriously mentally ill persons act as reasonably well-informed consumers is of questionable validity.

A further assumption is that 'output' is easily observed. Observability is crucial to the process of rewarding the physicians, hospitals and other components of the health care service system. For some of the chronically mentally ill, for example, it is not easy to develop measures of improved mental health status as a basis for paying providers while sustaining some reasonable cost control; until such measures are developed, however, there will be pressure from cost-conscious health care system planners to restrict the resources used in treatment.

Simply put, efficient use of resources in health care, including mental health care, requires balancing two distinct considerations—the social costs of illness, which are the benefits of better health—against the costs of providing the services that will produce those benefits. In the remainder of this chapter I will examine both costs and benefits of devoting more resources to treating the mentally ill.

The social cost of mental illness

The costs to society of mental illness depend on how mental illness is defined and measured. For the USA, for example, a recent comprehensive estimate of social costs separates the costs of drug abuse and alcohol abuse from those of mental illness (Rice *et al.*, 1991). As Table I shows, the consequences are enormous. The estimated costs of alcohol and drug abuse exceed the costs attributable to more narrowly defined mental illness. The more narrow mental health costs were $129 billion for the USA in 1988—about 2.5% of GNP—while the total of the three exceeded $273 billion—5% of GNP.

Table I.   Economic costs of alcohol and drug abuse and mental illness, 1988 (millions of dollars).

Cost	Total	Alcohol abuse	Drug abuse	Mental illness
Total	273 300	85 800	58 300	129 300
Core costs	207 708			
Direct (ADM specialty and federal institutions, short-stay hospitals, office-based physicians, other professional services, nursing homes, drugs and support costs.	65 592			
Indirect (Morbidity for institutionalized and non-institutionalized persons, and mortality[a])	142 116			
Other related costs (*Direct*: crime, motor vehicle crashes, fire destruction, and social welfare administration *Indirect*: victims of crime, incarceration, crime careers, and family caregiving)	62 859			
Special disease groups (AIDS and fetal alcohol syndrome)	5 466			

[a] Discounted at 6%.
Note: ADM = alcohol and drug abuse and mental illness.
   Source: Adapted from Rice, D.P., Kelman, S. and Miller, L.S., Estimates of economic costs of alcohol and drug abuse and mental illness, 1985 and 1988. *Public Health Reports*, May–June 1991, **106**, No. 3, 280–292.

The composition of these costs is important to understand, as social costs cannot be equated with monetary payments. Indeed, of the estimated total social costs of $273 billion shown in Table I, only 24% ($66 billion) involves payments for health services—physicians, drugs, hospitals, nursing homes, etc. More than 52% ($142 billion) of the total social cost consists of losses of productivity from the ill people, while the balance consists of adverse consequences that affect the economic system but do not involve health care resources (i.e., crime, motor vehicle accidents and fires).

Direct treatment costs and 'indirect' lost productivity costs have been estimated for Germany and Sweden, as well as for the USA. While the total cost of mental illness has been estimated at over 3.5% of the gross domestic product (GDP)* in Sweden, the cost in Germany is relatively far smaller, at 0.5%. In both countries the lost productivity is a major form of cost of mental illness—constituting 36% of the total social cost in Germany and 67% in Sweden (Table II).

These costs bring about the potential benefits from programmes that prevent or successfully treat mental illness. Note, though, that they are the benefits from eliminating mental illness; it is by no means clear, however, that a reduction of, say, 20% in the number of mentally ill persons would bring about a 20% reduction in the social costs, since it may well be that the more socially costly cases of chronic mental illness are also the more difficult to treat. The fundamental point is that the social costs of mental illness, no matter how large they may be, tell us little or nothing that is relevant for public policy without information about the costs of reducing those social costs—that is, the cost of obtaining those benefits.

Table II.   Economic costs of mental illness as a percentage of gross domestic product in the USA and the Federal Republic of Germany, 1980, and in Sweden, 1975.

	Germany	Sweden	USA
Total cost	0.46%	3.58%	1.13%
Direct cost	0.29	1.16	0.74
Indirect cost	0.16	2.42	0.39
Morbidity	0.11	2.36	0.33
Mortality[a]	0.05	0.05	0.06

a Estimated costs of mortality are calculated using a discount rate of 4% in the German and Swedish studies, and 6% in the US study.

Sources:

Henke, K.-D. and Behrens, C.S., The economic cost of illness in the Federal Republic of Germany in the year 1980. *Health Policy*, **6**, 1986, 119–143.

Lindgren, B., *Costs of Illness in Sweden, 1964–1975*. Liber, Lund, 1981, p. 134.

Rice, D.P., Hodgson, T.A. and Kopstein, A.N., The economic costs of illnesses: a replication and update. *Health Care Financing Review*, **7**, 1985, 61–80.

US Department of Health and Human Services, Health Care Financing Administration, *Health Care Financing Review*, 1989 Annual Supplement, p. 190.

* The GDP is a slightly different measure of national output from GNP; the difference between the two is the treatment of the country's imports.

I turn next to evidence about the ways in which mental illness imposes costs on society. Then, in the subsequent section I illustrate the use of benefit–cost analysis, which relates the social costs of mental illness to the costs of reducing them.

Social costs

The social costs of mental illness take a wide variety of forms. Many do not involve payment of money, and many are borne outside the mental health system. For example, mental illness imposes stress and anxiety on family members, which frequently do not appear in monetary form. Some social costs, such as family members' time lost from work, do involve financial losses, but they are sometimes thought of as costs of absenteeism or non-participation in the labour-force, rather than costs of mental illness. Similarly, mental illness imposes burdens on society broadly, through its effects on crime and law enforcement; although such costs are imposed on the criminal justice system they are

Table III.   Types of costs and benefits.

Costs	Benefits

1. Primary treatment
    MMHI
        Inpatient
        Outpatient
        Experimental centre programme
2. Secondary treatment
    Social service agencies
        Other hospitals (non-MMHI)
        Sheltered workshops
        Other community agencies
        Private medical providers
3. Law enforcement and illegal activities
    Police
    Courts
    Probation and parole
    Property damage, human physical
    injury
4. Additional maintenance (food,
    housing, etc.)
5. Family burdens
    Property and wage losses
    Psychic losses
6. Burdens on other people (e.g.
    neighbours, co-workers)
7. Patient mortality
	1. Improved mental health
	2. Improved physical health
	3. Improved labour productivity
	4. Improved consumer decision-making
	    efficiency

Source: Weisbrod, B.A., Benefit–cost analysis of a controlled experiment: treating the mentally ill. *Journal of Human Resources,* **16,** No. 4, Fall 1981. Reproduced by permission of the University of Wisconsin Press, © 1981.

properly attributable to mental illness. Table III lists a wide variety of forms that the social costs (and benefits) of mental illness can and do take.

How should resources be allocated among treatment or prevention of mental illness, and treatment and prevention of various physical illnesses—or, for that matter, to education, highways, or private goods and services? Economic analysis can contribute to answering such questions by sharpening the issues and by marshalling relevant quantitative information.

Social costs versus social benefits

Evidence on the social *costs* of mental illness cannot guide public policy on the allocation of resources. Two further elements are needed to link data on the cost of mental illness to a policy recommendation. One is the *knowledge base*— the information, diagnostic capabilities, effectiveness of drugs, psychoanalysis, surgery, etc., and the other procedures and techniques for prevention, diagnosis and treatment. The other is the *cost of applying that knowledge*, which encompasses the effectiveness of particular resources in reducing the frequency or severity of mental illness.

Thus the large social costs of mental illness must be weighed against the ease or difficulty of reducing those costs. That depends, in turn, on the state of knowledge and the cost of utilizing it. If little is known about effective means for prevention or treatment, or if it is very costly to implement the knowledge, it may not be efficient to devote substantial sums of money to mental illness even if mental illness imposes large social costs. As knowledge grows and as costs fall, the benefit–cost balance shifts in favour of increased action.

The economics of prevention

Prevention of illness—mental or physical—is preferred to treatment. It does not follow, however, that prevention is more efficient once the differential costs of treatment and prevention are taken into account. The economics of mental illness prevention has been studied very little, but prevention of various physical illnesses has been examined for a number of particular diseases, with mixed conclusions. Vaccination against polio has been found to be highly cost-efficient (Weisbrod, 1971), but in other areas it has often been found to be extremely costly—e.g., mass screening for low-prevalence illnesses (Russell, 1986).

Efficiency of preventive measures requires the ability to identify the people most likely to develop a particular illness. The easier it is to determine whether a particular individual will fall victim to a specific illness, the lower the resource cost of preventing a case of an illness. Consider, for example, a particular technique (vaccine, surgery, counselling, etc.) that is known (a) to be completely effective in preventing a specific illness, and (b) to cost $100 per person treated. Assume, further, that (c) without using that technique, 0.1% of that population would contract the illness. It would be necessary to treat 1000 persons, at $100 each, for a total cost of $100 000, to prevent a single case. If, by contrast, the incidence of that illness was not 0.1% but 10%, the cost of preventing one case would be $100 × 10, or $1000. Note that when treatment, rather than prevention, is involved, it is known with virtual certainty that the person being treated does have the illness. Thus, while the advantages of prevention are obvious, it is the cost considerations that may lead public and private policy towards treatment rather than prevention.

In weighing the economic case for prevention relative to treatment, an important cost consideration is whether the technology involves custom production or mass production. A surgical technique, for example, will inevitably be costly, for it involves individualized production—a team of surgeons, nurses and other assistants working together to treat a single patient. The same is true of individual psychotherapy for the mentally ill. By contrast, a therapeutic drug can be produced by the millions in ways that take advantage of cost economies of large-scale production.

Incentives to develop new technologies for treatment and prevention of mental or other illnesses affect the pattern of technological change. (For an analysis of economic forces influencing incentives facing the research and development sector in the health area, see Weisbrod, 1991.) Indeed, the quite limited health insurance coverage in the USA for outpatient mental illness care has discouraged development of technologies for treating the mentally ill in a non-institutionalized setting. Despite the biased financial incentives towards treating the mentally ill in institutions, some major R&D advances in pharmaceuticals—particularly the psychotropic drugs—have had an enormous effect on the ways that the mentally ill are being treated. In the USA, the number of patients in mental hospitals plummeted by some 70% from its peak of 559 000 in 1955 to 216 000 in 1974 and 159 000 in 1987.*

The cost saving associated with treatment regimes that avoid hospitalization is clear. What is less clear, however, is whether those savings are offset by increased costs in non-hospital cost forms. I turn now to an illustration of a sophisticated economic benefit–cost analysis that compares a hospital-based therapeutic regime with a community-based programme that attempted to bring skilled professional resources to patients in a non-hospital setting. Both programmes involve treating the mentally ill, not preventing it. The goal in presenting this illustration is threefold: to highlight the relevance of both costs and benefits to efficient public policy development toward mental illness; to demonstrate the varied forms that costs and benefits take; and to show the feasibility

---

* *Statistical Abstract of the United States, 1990*, US Bureau of the Census, Table 181.

of careful, comprehensive evaluation of programmes for dealing with the large social costs of mental illness.

An applied benefit–cost analysis for treating the mentally ill

There is no single way of treating all the mentally ill. As a result, efficient resource allocation requires that we examine the costs and benefits of each treatment approach. In general, the treatment that brings the greatest excess of benefits over costs is the most efficient. 'Costs' consist of all disadvantages, which include the labour, capital and other resources required—whether or not payments are made for them—as well as adverse effects on outside parties. 'Benefits' consist of all advantages, which include favourable outcomes for the mentally ill patients—whether or not they are received in monetary form—as well as favourable effects on outside parties.

In the experiment to which I now turn, the total costs and benefits are estimated and then compared for two distinctly different approaches to treating the mentally ill. One is a traditional hospital-based programme, referred to here as the control programme (C). The second is a community-based experimental programme (E) involving active support of patients in an outpatient setting. The 1972–1975 experiment involved a random assignment, of 130 mentally ill patients between the ages of 18 and 62 with diagnoses other than severe organic brain syndrome or primary alcoholism, to either community treatment (E) or hospital treatment (C). Is such a community-based programme less costly and/ or more effective (i.e. socially beneficial)?

The essential characteristics of the E programme were as follows. (1) Hospitalization is virtually eliminated. (2) Members of the staff work with patients in their neighbourhoods, places of residence and places of employment, providing support and teaching the coping skills necessary to maintain a satisfactory community adjustment. (3) The staff attempt to minimize the number of patients dropping out of treatment prematurely and to maximize their engagement in jobs and other aspects of responsible, independent community living. Staff effort was also directed towards patients' families and community agencies. Meetings were held with family members to help guide (or in many cases to stop, at least temporarily) interactions detrimental to the patient's adjustment.

The C programme consisted of progressive short-term in-hospital treatment (generally lasting less than one month) plus traditional after-care provided by community mental health agencies. Patients assigned to the C group were screened immediately by a member of the hospital's acute treatment and were usually, though not always, admitted to the hospital.

E subjects, by contrast, did not enter the hospital at all (except in rare emergency situations). Instead, they received the 'community living' treatment for 14 months, after which they had no further contact with the experimental unit staff.

Viewed from an economic perspective, the E programme confronts patients with more of the real costs of their actions than does the C-type approach. Under the C-type programme, a mentally ill person who does not behave in a socially acceptable manner on the job, in his or her rooming house or in the community is not punished but, to the contrary, is typically 'rewarded' by being placed in a protected and subsidized hospital environment which the individual prefers. Indeed, it is not uncommon for such persons intentionally to do things, including violating minor laws, so as to be sent back to the hospital. Thus, behaviour that imposes external costs is actually rewarded! (For more details on the experiment and the benefit–cost analysis, see Weisbrod, 1983.)

This experiment, while undertaken some years ago, is worth examining because it involved random assignment, which is extremely important for evaluation purposes but has become far more difficult, legally, to arrange in subsequent years. The experiment was also unusual in the comprehensiveness and detail of its analysis of benefits and costs.

Data collection

Data were collected for the 65 persons in each group at baseline (admission) and, for most variables, at four-monthly intervals during the subsequent year. Family members of a subsample of patients were also interviewed at the time of the patient's admission and again four months later in order to assess the effects of the patient's illness on family. Information about patient contacts with various public and private agencies were generally verified with the agencies involved, and those agencies were also contacted to ascertain the (average) costs of the services provided.

Budget constraints limited the scope of the experiment in its duration, and in our ability to vary and control different combinations of variables. Thus, for example, the experimental design permits only conjecture regarding whether the E programme's benefits or its costs per patient year would be different if the duration of the programme were longer or shorter, or if some specific elements of the E programme were altered or dropped.

Table III, which lists the forms of costs and benefits that would be desirable to measure, is the basis for our efforts to develop quantitative measures. Slightly reorganized, the measures and their estimated values are presented in Table IV. We turn now to those estimates. Table IV provides monetary values for some forms of costs and benefits, quantitative but non-monetary data where valuation is not feasible, and leaves blank spaces or question marks for particular forms of costs or benefits for which no quantitative information is available (Table VI shows the actual quantity units that lie behind the pecuniary data in Table IV. When multiplied by the respective prices, these quantities yielded the dollar amounts shown in Table IV.)

Table IV. Costs and benefits per patient for 12 months following admission to experiment.

	Control group (C)	Experimental group (E)	E − C
Costs for which monetary estimates have been made			
Direct treatment costs			
Mendota Mental Health Institute (MMHI)			
Inpatient	$ 3069	$ 94	$−3002**
Outpatient	42	0	−42**
Experimental centre programme	0	4704	4704†
Total	$ 3138	$ 4798	$ 1660†
Indirect treatment costs			
Social service agencies			
Other hospitals (non-MMHI)	$ 1744	$ 646	$−1098**
Sheltered workshops			
Madison Opportunity Centre, Inc., and Goodwill Industries	91	870	779**
Other community agencies			
Dane County Mental Health Centre	$ 55	$ 50	$ −5
Dane County Social Services	41	25	−16**
State Department of Vocational Rehabilitation	185	209	24[a]
Visiting Nurse Service	0	23	23**
State Employment Service	4	3	−1*
Private medical providers	22	12	−10[e]
Total	$ 2142	$ 1838	$ −304
Law enforcement costs			
Overnights in jail	$ 159	$ 152	$ −7[b]
Court contacts	17	12	−5[b]
Probation and parole	189	143	−46
Police contacts	44	43	−1[b]
Total	$ 409	$ 350	$ −59†
Maintenance costs	$ 1487	$ 1035	$ −452
Family burden costs			
Lost earnings due to the patient	$ 120	$ 72	$ −48[c,d]
Total costs for which monetary estimates have been made	$ 7296	$ 8093	$ 797†
Other costs			
Other family burden costs			
Percentage of families reporting physical illness due to the patient	25%	14%	−11%[c]
Percentage of family members experiencing emotional strain due to the patient	48%	25%	−23%[c,i]

Table IV.   (*cont.*)

	Control group (C)	Experimental group (E)	E – C
Burdens on other people (e.g. neighbours, co-workers)	?	?	?
Total illegal activity costs	1.0	0.8	−0.2[b]
Total number of arrests for felony	0.2	0.2	0.0[b]
Patient mortality costs (percentage dying during the year)			
Suicide	1.5	1.5	0
Natural causes	0	4.6	4.6
Benefits for which monetary estimates have been made			
Earnings[f]			
From competitive employment	1136	2169	1033**[g]
From sheltered workshops	32	195	163**[g]
Total	$ 1168	$ 2364	$ 1196†
Other benefits			
Labour market behaviour			
Days of competitive employment per year	77	127	50[g]
Days of sheltered employment per year	10	89	79[g]
Percentage of days missed from job	3%	7%	4%[g]
No. beneficial job changes	2	3	1[h]
No. detrimental job changes	2	2	0[h]
Improved consumer decision-making			
Insurance expenditures	$ 33	$ 56	$ 23[g]
Percentage of group having savings accounts	27%	34%	7%
Improved mental health status (See Table V)			
Summary			
Valued benefits	$ 1168	$ 2364	$ 1196
Valued costs	7296	8093	797
Net (benefits – costs)	$–6128	$–5729	$ 399†

* Significant at the 0.10 level.
** Significant at the 0.05 level.
† Significance not tested, as the number is a sum of means.
[a] Data from the Department of Vocational Rehabilitation (DRV) were available only for the 28-month study period as a whole, which included the follow-up period after the experiment. The per patient costs presented are 12/28, or 43% of the 28-month data, reflecting average cost for one year. The figures reflect some double counting because much of the DVR expenditures go for payments to other agencies that are included in this section of the table. We have been able to account for, and to exclude, DVR payments to the sheltered workshops but not, for

(*continued over*)

Costs

The per diem cost of inpatient care at the state mental hospital (Mendota Mental Health Institute, MMHI) was examined with special care because it was likely to be quantitatively dominant. As estimated by the State of Wisconsin (and by governments generally), this cost is incomplete in three respects, each of which led me to adjust the state-provided costs statistic: (1) the opportunity cost of the land on which the hospital is located had been disregarded; (2) the depreciation of the hospital buildings was based on historical cost rather than the far greater replacement cost; and (3) research carried out at MMHI was included in the per diem cost figure for the hospital. The per diem cost estimate by the state, approximately $70 in 1973, was adjusted upwards to allow for an opportunity cost of 8% on the estimated value of the land and the depreciated replacement cost of the physical plant, and it was adjusted slightly downward to account for research activities, which are not appropriately includable as treatment costs. The result was an increase to $100 in the MMHI per diem cost, our estimate of long-run marginal (and average) cost of treatment at that institution.

These adjustments made the MMHI treatment cost data more comparable with the experimental centre cost data, for the latter also excluded research expenditures while including commercial rental payments for the centre, and these payments presumably reflected a normal return on both the land and the depreciated replacement value of the physical structure.

C group patients also made use of facilities for outpatient treatment at MMHI. The average cost of such a contact was estimated by MMHI staff to average $10 per patient visit.

---

example, to hospitals. The $24 difference is biased upward by the omission of counselling expenses attributable only to C group members.

  [b] These data derived from agency or patient reports on the number of contacts, patient reports being used only when it was not possible, or was excessively costly to obtain the relevant information from the agency. Estimates per contact were obtained from the agency.

  [c] These figures are derived from interviews conducted four months after admission with 22 families of E group patients and 18 families of C group patients (34% of the E group, 27% of the C group). The other families were not interviewed because: (a) they lived outside Dane County (23% of each group); (b) the subject or the family refused to cooperate (12% of the E group, 22% of the C group); or (c) the relative could not be contacted (31% of the E group, 28% of the C group). The questionnaire examined the families' experience in the two weeks preceding the interview only, and, with some trepidation, these figures are inflated to an annual average. The reduced sample size and the single interview yielded data which must be interpreted with caution.

  [d] These figures were derived by multiplying the number of days family members missed work because of the patient by a daily wage of $24 (or $3 an hour).

  [e] These figures include fees for physicians, psychologists and nurses but exclude any associated laboratory fees.

  [f] Earnings do not include value of fringe benefits, if there were any.

  [g] These data are derived from patient reports and as such are subject to misreporting. Patient reports were used only when it was not possible (or was excessively costly) to obtain the relevant information from an independent source. In some cases, when an interviewer suspected faulty reporting, individual spot checks were made with the agency in question; agencies that were not able to provide us with information on all patients were sometimes able to provide it on this spot check basis.

  [h] These are our judgements, based on examination of patient reports.

  [i] These are interviewers' assessments.

  Source: Weisbrod, B.A., Benefit–cost analysis of a controlled experiment: treating the mentally ill. *Journal of Human Resources*, **16**, No. 4, Fall 1981. Reproduced by permission of the University of Wisconsin Press, © 1981.

'Secondary' (or 'indirect') treatment includes a wide range of medical and related helping services by various agencies, institutions and professions and available to both groups of patients outside of their respective primary treatment facilities. The category includes other hospitals and psychiatric institutions, halfway houses, sheltered workshops, visiting nurses, counselling and educational services, etc.

Another form of social cost that may vary with the treatment mode involves law enforcement. We were able to obtain data from patient interviews on the number of police and court contacts, the number of nights spent in jail, and the number of contacts with probation and parole officers. Reported contacts with the Police Department and the County Sheriff's Office were verified, but those with other departments were not. The costs per contact and overnight were obtained by methods essentially the same as those used for secondary treatment costs.

Patient 'maintenance' is required simply to live and thus, it might be argued, should be excluded from that table. On the other hand, the E programme involved encouraging independent living arrangements; therefore, the resulting higher level of maintenance costs is a real cost of this treatment mode. Thus, in principle, we should include as real costs only the incremental maintenance costs attributable to the E programme. (For an analysis of the quantitative substitution between costs incurred in the patient's home and in the hospital, see Franks, 1990.) In practice, however, it is extraordinarily difficult to identify these additional costs. In the final analysis, all 'maintenance' costs—for housing, meals, clothing, etc.—were counted as costs, which included those provided in kind as well as in money form.

Patients interact with other persons in a wide range of settings. While we could not obtain information on all such interactions, I have examined two categories of individuals for whom these external (to the patient) costs are likely to be particularly great: members of the patients' immediate families, and other people who have suffered because of illegal or at least disruptive behaviour on the part of patients. Data on these burdens were obtained both from interviews with patient families after four months, and from records of courts and law enforcement agencies.

In the interviews, family members were asked whether or not they had experienced work or school absences, disruption of domestic or social routines, trouble with neighbours, or stress-related physical ailments as a result of the patient's illness.* They were also asked if the patient's illness had forced them to purchase services formerly provided by the patient, whether they had paid for psychiatric treatment or medication received by the patient, and whether they

---

* Information obtained from the family burden interview is limited in two major respects. The size of the sample is small (49 out of 130) and the follow-up period (four months) is short. (Budgetary constraints and concern about the burden imposed by the interviews themselves limited the number of follow-up interviews.)

had given cash or large non-cash gifts to the patient. The interviewer then rated each family as suffering a 'severe', 'moderate', 'mild' or 'no' burden from the patient's illness.

Benefits

Improving the mental health of patients is the primary goal of any illness treatment programme. Such improvements may well increase the productivity of patients as workers or their efficiency as consumers. They may also bring external benefits to family members and society more generally, in the forms discussed above. But to many people these results are less important than the benefits of patients' feeling better and being more satisfied with life.

In the quantitative work presented below, there are no pecuniary values for improvement in the state of a subject's mental health. This is one of the variables for which quantitative but non-pecuniary indicators seem most appropriate. Three such indicators are used: (1) objective measures of quality of life, such as the number of leisure-time social groups the subject reported having attended in the month preceding the interview (at four, eight and 12 months);

Table V.   Mental health indicators, E and C subjects.

Indicators	Significance
I. *Symptomatology*	
4 months	E group was significantly (0.05) less symptomatic on 4 of the 13 measures (including global illness); on the other 9, there were no significant differences
8 months	E group was significantly (0.05) less symptomatic on 4 of the 13 measures (including global illness); on the other 9, there were no significant differences
12 months	E group was significantly (0.05) less symptomatic on 7 of the 13 measures (including global illness); on the other 6, there were no significant differences
II. *Social relationships*	
4 months	E group had significantly (0.05) more (2.1 v. 0.7)
8 months	E group had significantly (0.05) more (1.7 v. 0.8)
12 months	E group had significantly (0.05) more (1.9 v. 0.6)
III. *Patient satisfaction with life*	
4 months	No significant difference between E and C
8 months	No significant difference between E and C
12 months	E group significantly (0.05) higher mean score

Source: Weisbrod, B.A., Benefit–cost analysis of a controlled experiment: treating the mentally ill. *Journal of Human Resources*, **16**, No. 4, Fall 1981. Reproduced by permission of the University of Wisconsin Press, © 1981.

Table VI. Quantities of services or resources utilized per patient, experimental and control groups, for 12 months following admission to experiment.

Costs	Group C	Group E
Direct treatment costs		
Mendota Mental Health Institute (MMHI)		
Inpatient days	31.4	3.0
Outpatient days	6.1	0
Indirect treatment costs		
Social service agencies		
Other hospitals (not MMHI)	—	—
Sheltered workshop days	5.6	52.3
Other community agencies		
Dane County Mental Health Services Board (contacts)	3.8	6.8
Dane County Social Services (contacts)	2.8	1.8
State Employment Service (days)	0.5	0.2
Private medical providers (contacts)	1.9	1.3
Law enforcement costs		
Overnights in jail	15.9	15.7
Court contacts	0.3	0.2
Probation and parole (occurrences)	2.2	1.5
Police contacts (arrests)	0.5	0.7

Source: Weisbrod, B.A., Benefit–cost analysis of a controlled experiment: treating the mentally ill. *Journal of Human Resources,* **16**, No. 4, Fall 1981. Reproduced by permission of the University of Wisconsin Press, © 1981.

(2) a trained interviewer's judgement of the presence or absence of various symptoms of mental illness, plus an overall 'global illness' assessment; and (3) the subject's own assessment of how satisfied he or she is with life in general (living situation, friends, food, work, etc.). Empirical results for each of these are presented in Table V.

A potential benefit of any treatment programme for mentally ill adults is an improvement in a patient's lifetime ability to function as an economic producer. A full accounting for increased productivity would encompass not only increases in productivity in the organized market, but also in unpaid work in the home, as well as increased investment in human capital (perhaps via education) which can be expected to increase future productivity. Data on work experience and earnings were obtained from the quarterly interviews with patients. Information on sheltered workshop employment and earnings was provided directly by the workshops.

Increased work stability is another potential benefit from an effective mental illness treatment programme. That is, wages, either actual or imputed, are not the only useful measure of effects on productivity of the two treatment modes. Work stability provides some evidence of future productivity, and hence can serve as an indicator of expected earnings beyond the period of the experiment. We measured the differences in this dimension of job performance for the C and E group patients in two ways: by absenteeism and by the number of 'beneficial' and 'detrimental' job changes made by the patient. Any statistically significant differences in the number of beneficial changes (e.g. moving to a job with a higher wage rate) and detrimental changes (e.g. being fired) can reasonably be treated as evidence of differences in the effectiveness of the two treatment programmes.

Another potential benefit of a successful treatment programme is an improvement in the subject's ability to manage his or her finances. Indicators of such benefits, let alone monetary values for them, are difficult to devise. I present below information on two indicators, both of which are simply suggestive. One is the subject's expenditure on insurance, reflecting the patient's attention to the future and its uncertainties. There is reason to believe that, within limits, increased attention to the future is a sign of improved mental health. It should be noted, however, that while the expenditures on insurance may be an *indicator* of improved health and, hence, of social benefits, such expenditures do not themselves constitute benefits that are additive to benefits in the form of, say, added earnings.

A second indicator of more efficient consumer behaviour for the mentally ill is saving behaviour. Again, within limits, increased saving reflects an increased, and healthy, concern for the future. These two indicators are far from satisfactory. They are included primarily as illustrations of a class of benefit variables that is conceptually relevant but easily overlooked—the effect of improved mental health on the efficiency of individuals' decision-making. By including them explicitly, the benefit–cost analyst underscores for the policy-maker the necessity of making judgements about their importance.

Several findings in Table IV are worthy of being highlighted. (1) Average total dollar costs are of substantial magnitude—$7300–$8100 per patient-year—whichever treatment approach is used, and only about half of the total is in the form of primary treatment costs. (2) Average total dollar costs of mental illness, including both treatment and non-treatment costs, are some 10% higher for the E programme than for the C programme—$8093 versus $7296. (3) As anticipated, the forms of costs are quite different for the two treatment approaches. For example, the E programme entails 50% greater direct treatment costs—$4798 per patient compared with $3138 per C programme patient. Similarly, while there is only about a 15% difference (in favour of the E group) in total indirect treatment costs, some components of indirect costs show a much greater difference. For example, the 'other hospital' component of E programme costs is some 60% smaller than that of the C programme—about $650 per patient for the E group. Sheltered workshop costs are nine times as large annually for the E group—$870 versus $91.

(4) Although spending more time in the community, the average E patient did

not have more contacts with the law. They also imposed fewer burdens on their families, although the differences are not statistically significant.

(5) There is no statistically significant difference in the number of deaths from natural causes, and no difference at all in the number of suicides. Table IV intentionally stops short of placing a monetary value on lost human lives.

Turning to benefits, we sought operational measures of whether each treatment programme helped patients to 'feel better' and to be more 'productive' members of society. Table IV shows that (6) E group patients performed substantially better in the labour market, as measured by differences in mean earnings. The experimental group averaged more than twice the earnings of control group members, and almost all of the excess was from competitive employment rather than from sheltered workshops.

Mental health status, as judged by outside observers, was affected differently by the two programmes. Since there is no single measure or indicator of mental health, we used multiple measures. One approach involved a trained observer meeting with patients and reporting on the presence or absence of various adverse symptoms. (7) The top panel of Table V shows that the E group averaged fewer symptoms at the four- and eight-month interviews, and still fewer at the 12-month interview. These findings are even more striking when it is realized that the E group was actually more symptomatic at the time of admission to the experiment.

Panel 2 of Table V presents another indicator of mental health status— number of social relationships. Since the mentally ill tend to withdraw from social contacts, more frequent contacts are interpreted as favourable. (8) E group members consistently had more social relationships than did C group patients.

Mental health status as judged by patients is a third indicator of improved mental health. Panel 3 of Table V reports that (9) although there was no significant difference between E and C patients' reported 'satisfaction with life' after four and eight months, the E group was significantly more satisfied by the end of month 12.

All of these findings indicate that E patients, who were spending a significantly greater proportion of their time in the community, were becoming better adjusted socially than were their C group counterparts, and they were experiencing greater improvement in their quality of life.

These quantitative findings show that the danger of mistaking a shift in the *form* of cost for a change in the *level* of cost is a real one. If we had neglected, for example, to examine the costs of providing sheltered workshop services, we would have found that average total costs were virtually identical for the two programmes, whereas, because the workshops were used far more by E patients, the E programme proved to be 10% more costly in total. And if we had limited our attention to hospitals in the county rather than extending it to 'out of town' hospitals, we would have underestimated the C programme per patient cost by $808 per year while underestimating the E programme cost by only $264 per year.

The quantitative findings also show that the somewhat greater cost of the E programme brought an even greater increase in benefits. Table IV shows that the E programme has added benefits in the form of labour market earnings alone that almost equal the added E programme costs. When the unvalued mental health benefits in Table IV are considered, the net advantage to the E programme becomes apparent, assuming these benefits are given any reasonable value.

Summing up the quantitative findings, we find that the experimental programme: (a) cost an additional $800 per patient year, but in return produced increased productivity (as measured by earnings) of at least $500; (b) showed evidence of enhancing the planning and decision-making skills of patients (insurance and savings behaviour); (c) decreased patient mental illness symptomatology; and (d) increased patient satisfaction with life. The evidence suggests that the community-based E approach would justify the added costs, assuming the B–C relationship estimated in a single-year experiment would hold over time.

Concluding remarks

In the debate over national health insurance, scant attention has been given to mental illness and even less to the choice among alternative types of delivery systems. The research reported here suggests that, except for emergency situations, hospitalization of the mentally ill may be less effective than community-based treatment of approximately equal cost.

These findings point at the potential for applying benefit–cost analysis to programmes for treating the mentally ill. They also highlight the fact that since alternative therapies exist and are likely to be differentially effective for different types of patients, what is needed for wise public policy is evaluation of various therapies for various patient populations.

In the context of the continuing policy debate over deinstitutionalization of the mentally ill, it is important to note that the generally favourable effects found in this experiment did not result from the mere 'dumping' of mentally ill persons from mental hospitals and into the community. To the contrary, the community-based alternative reflected an aggressive effort to bring a wide range of treatment and helping resources to the aid of the non-hospitalized mentally ill. The benefit–cost analysis of that multidimensional effort has disclosed that its benefits, viewed from a variety of perspectives, are sizeable. Unfortunately, so are its costs.

The benefit–cost framework for programme evaluation in mental health care underscores a number of important points. (1) Studies showing the large aggregate social costs of mental illness are striking, but they provide no direct guidance for deciding how many resources to allocate for either treating or preventing mental illness. (2) Incentives operating in the mental health area, as with health care more generally, have implicitly encouraged the development and utilization of resources for treating the ill rather than preventing the illness. (3) Efficient resource use implies that costs and benefits of various specific types of mental health programmes be identified, quantified and compared.

In an environment of growing political concern about the rising costs of health care, treatment of the mentally ill is also falling prey to cost containment pressures; in the process, low-cost technologies, such as embodied in relatively inexpensive pharmaceuticals, will seem to be attractive, while labour-intensive long-term regimes involving hospitalization or individual psychotherapies will be restricted. Quantitative benefit–cost analysis can influence judgements about the efficiency of alternative therapies by showing whether programmes that appear to bring cost *reductions* are actually doing so or are merely *shifting* costs to other people. Meaningful benefit–cost analysis calls for close collaboration of economists and mental health specialists.

At any point in time there is a given state of knowledge about the means for treating or preventing mental illness. The economic efficiency of deploying that knowledge—that is, of devoting increased resources to mental illness—depends on the severity of the mental illness problem (the social costs) and the costs and effectiveness of utilizing the means available for dealing with the problem.

In the long run, these variables change. In particular, research and development can have massive effects on knowledge about ways to prevent and treat mental illness. The forms, directions and magnitude of R&D, moreover, are influenced heavily by financial incentives; these operate in large part through mental health care finance systems, and these systems have provided incentives for treatment more than prevention. They have also provided incentives that have driven total health care and mental health care system costs upward dramatically, and the current world-wide reaction is now focusing on cost containment rather than on quality enhancement. The implications for the mental health sector are immense: high-cost treatment approaches such as long-term hospitalization and extensive psychotherapy will be under growing pressure, while drug therapies will be increasingly favoured by cost-conscious finance authorities. The swing of the political pendulum underscores the need for examining both benefits and costs of health and mental health care. To an economist, the problem is to balance concerns with cost and concerns about the plight of the mentally ill.

Acknowledgement

I thank Laura Connolly and Lew Segal for research assistance, and Audrey Chambers for editorial assistance.

References

Franks DD (1990) Economic contribution of families caring for severe and persistent mental illness. *Admin Policy Ment Health* **18**, 9–18.

Rice DP, Kelman S and Miller LS (1991) Estimates of economic costs of alcohol and drug abuse and mental illness, 1985 and 1988. *Public Health Rep* **106**, 280–292.

Russell L (1986) *Is Prevention Better than Cure?* Washington, DC: Brookings Institution.

Weisbrod B (1971) Costs and benefits of medical research: a case study of poliomyelitis. *J Political Economy* **79**, 527–544.

Weisbrod BA (1983) A guide to the benefit–cost analysis, as seen through a controlled experiment in treating the mentally ill. *J Health Polit Policy Law* **7**, 805–845.

Weisbrod B (1991) The health care quadrilemma: an essay on technological change, insurance, quality of care, and cost containment. *J Econ Lit* **29**, 523–552.

3

Economic studies of the treatment of depressive illness

Bengt Jönsson and Paul Bebbington

Introduction

The overall social impact of any medical condition depends on its frequency and its effects. Depressive illness is a very common condition. It is likely that in most communities, certainly those in the industrialized world, the prevalence of major depressive disorder is of the order of 2½–3% (Bebbington, 1992).

Depressive illness forms a continuum from relatively mild disorders to very severe psychotic conditions. However, even less severe depressive disorders will impair the social functioning of those suffering from them (Paykel *et al.*, 1978; Weissman, 1978; Hurry *et al.*, 1987). The result is that depressed people require considerable support from families, and if the condition is at all persistent the degree of burden experienced by relatives is often considerable (Fadden *et al.*, 1987a,b). Thus, in societal terms, depressive illness is of great significance. The cost of treating it is also likely to be significant.

Although the social impact of depressive illness has been quantified, it has rarely been translated into economic terms. It can nevertheless be anticipated that a condition which is so common and which has such marked social consequences will consume considerable economic resources.

In this chapter, we first calculate the overall cost for treating depression in the UK in a given year, using a range of published and unpublished statistics. This provides a context for an analysis of the cost-effectiveness of pharmacological treatment. Although it is always important to choose cost-effective treatments, it

Health Economics of Depression. Edited by B. Jönsson and J. Rosenbaum

is particularly so where the overall sources committed to the treatment of the condition are high.

We then move on to develop a model of the pharmacological treatment of depressive illness which allows us to estimate the relative cost-effectiveness of an established tricyclic antidepressant and one of the newer *selective serotonin reuptake inhibitors* (SSRIs).

Costing the treatment of depressive illness

The cost of an illness to the national economy comprises both direct and indirect costs. The direct costs are those of detecting, treating, preventing, rehabilitating and caring for the sufferers. In theory, this should include all the costs of care, whether provided by the health services or other agencies. In practice, there is a limit to what can be identified and measured. Thus studies have concentrated on the cost of hospitalization, outpatient care, general practitioner care and drugs. Costs should be included in the total regardless of who pays: the patient, the government, or some other institution.

The indirect costs are those that come about because sufferers are unable to maintain their economic roles. This is related to the short-term effects of illness, and the consequences of permanent disability and premature death. There may also be a further element due to the loss of production of family members taking care of the patients.

There are several problems, both general and particular, connected with the measurement of such costs in depressive illness. So, for example, it is difficult to know if the salaries used to calculate lost production accurately measure the actual value of lost production. There is also a specific difficulty with depressive illness, in that one of its consequences is suicide, and suicide is coded under a different part of the International Classification of Disease. It is thus impossible to include the cost of suicide within the cost of depressive illness. Because of these difficulties, there has only been one attempt to estimate the indirect costs of depressive illness: an American study by Stoudemire and his colleagues (1986). Although we have reservations about this study, it does make the quite credible suggestion that indirect costs greatly exceed the direct costs of treating the illness. The authors claim that indirect costs exceed direct costs by a factor of 7:1; this value is probably of the right order of magnitude.

For good practical reasons we therefore elected in our own study to concentrate on the *direct* costs of treating depression. We chose the cost-of-illness method based on the Human Capital Theory (Hodgson and Meiners, 1982). This is well established and straightforward, but decisions have to be made over epidemiological options. One of these involves whether to base the study on the prevalence or on the incidence of the illness. These two approaches result in rather different sorts of information. If we wish to know the implications in cost terms of the emergence of new cases of depressive illness, we require to know the number of new cases appearing within a given period, and then examine cost implications for the rest of the expected lifetime of the individual sufferer. This does have the advantage of identifying the consequences of changing the occurrence of the disease. This means that it is particularly appropriate for the investigation of preventive treatments, where the benefits can be measured as the number of cases avoided.

However, it is equally valid to enquire about the yearly costs of treating an illness. This is a way of evaluating its impact on total annual health care expenditure. In this instance, the cost of illness is that due to the prevalence of the disease, and takes account of all cases existing during the given year. The resources used for prevention, treatment and rehabilitation within that year can then be calculated.

As we were more concerned with the benefits of effective treatment than with the prevention of depressive illness, it seemed best to estimate the cost of depressive illness based on prevalence.

In order to this, we used a top-down approach, whereby we identified the total national cost of illness specifically due to depressive illness rather than to other conditions. So, for example, we identified the total number of hospital bed days devoted to patients suffering from depressive disorders. This approach has the advantage of relating to the total cost of treating depressive illness in the country as a whole. It does require good data on the use of health care resources in relation to the specific diagnostic group, and for depressive illness there are likely to be inaccuracies due to under-reporting of diagnoses.

In our study we defined depression as codes 296 and 311 of the International Classification of Disease (ICD-9, World Health Organization, 1978). This definition is not wholly equivalent to the same-numbered categories in the Diagnostic and Statistic Manual of Mental Disorders (DSM-III-R, American Psychiatric Association, 1987) as the ICD-9 contains the additional category 300.4: neurotic depression. Unfortunately, the Department of Health in the UK does not provide separate figures for this category, which is included under neuroses. The calculation therefore underestimates the true cost burden of depression. Incidence data and estimates of costs were obtained from the Department of Health, the Office for the Population Censuses and Surveys, and the British Medical Association, using published and unpublished data.

Table I summarizes the data used for the calculation of the direct cost of depression in the UK. It shows the unit cost data and the year of origin of the information, together with an uprating to 1990 prices. Estimates have been extrapolated to the country as a whole, on the assumption that the uptake of services is geographically uniform and constant over time.

The overall cost of treating depressive illness was estimated to be £222 million. The breakdown of these costs is provided in Figure 1. It requires comment. The drug bill is less than a quarter of the total, while the cost of hospital

Table I.   Direct costs for depression (ICD-9 codes 296 and 311) in the UK.

Type of outpatient care	Number	Unit cost (£) (year)	Source of data	Unit cost at 1990 prices (£)
Outpatient visits	243 000	29.22 (1987)	Health and Personal Social Statistics Report (1985) and South Manchester Health Authority[c]	36
ECT sessions	109 800	60 (1989)	Department of Health (unpublished data)[d] and South Manchester Health Authority	60
Psychotherapy sessions	54 105	45.45 (1988)	Department of Health (unpublished data)[c] and South Manchester Health Authority	50
GP visits (number)	3 119 685	—	Royal College of General Practitioners (1986)	—
GP visit based on 15-minute consultation (costs)	—	—	British Medical Association (unpublished data)	20
Hospital day	—	119.42 (1989)	Costing returns, Department of Health (unpublished data)	132
Hospital admissions[a]	50 214	—	Department of Health and Social Security and Office of Population Censuses and Surveys (1985)	—
Drugs[b]	—	41 722 200 (1988)	Prescription Pricing Authority/Department of Health (1988)	—

[a] Mean length of stay = 14.16 days (Department of Health and Social Security and Office of Population Censuses and Surveys, 1987).
[b] Prescriptions for ICD-9 codes 296 and 311.
[c] Costing returns, 1987–1989 (personal communication, Department of Health, 1991).
[d] Hospital Episode Statistical System.

admission for depressive illness on its own approaches £100 million. In a way, hospital admission can be seen as an admission of failure, insofar as prompt and effective treatment for depression ought in the 1990s to be able to prevent many episodes of inpatient treatment. It is within this context we must see the relative cost-effectiveness of pharmacological treatments.

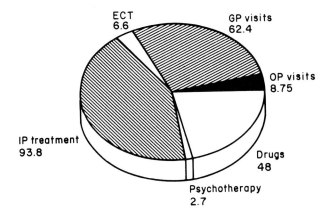

Figure 1.   Direct costs of treating depression in the UK.

Cost of illness methodology provides a framework for evaluating the cost of new treatment by identifying where the main costs of treatment arises: such studies can quantify the potential for reducing costs with more effective treatment.

The method has, however, been criticized. One ground for criticism is that, as it is impossible to avoid all the costs of treating a disease, it is difficult to know the extent to which new treatments will improve things. It has also been argued that cost of illness methods show a bias in the favour of the working population. However, this relates more to the indirect costs of illness, not direct costs as in our study. A major problem for our purposes was that the definition of depression does not include ICD category 300.4 (neurotic depression). It is known that the inclusion of this category increases the number of admissions due to depressive illness by around 25% (Bebbington, 1987). The disorders included under this rubric probably lie towards the mild end of the spectrum, and are therefore relatively unlikely to result in hospital admissions. It thus seems likely that the discrepancy would be even greater for outpatients and for general practice attendances.

There are very few other studies of the costs of treating depression. Stoudemire and his colleagues (1986) offer a systematic attempt to estimate the cost of depression to the US economy at 1980 prices. They made separate evaluations of levels of morbidity and mortality, direct and indirect treatment costs, years of activity lost, and years of life lost. They estimated that the direct costs of treating depression in the USA was $2.1 billion per year. However, the costs also include $10 billion per year in total morbidity costs of lost productivity, and $4.2 billion as the total loss from increased mortality. The authors thought that these figures were lower bound estimates, and we would agree.

The value that we arrived at for direct costs is likely to underestimate all but the drug costs. The real figure lies between our value of £200+ million and perhaps £400 million. Allowing for the different size of population in health care costs, this is actually quite close to the estimate of Stoudemire and colleagues (1986).

Recently, an independent calculation of the direct costs of treating depression in the UK has been made by West (1992). He too used a top-down approach. He took the total cost of mental health care at 1986–7 prices as just under £1200 million. Depressive diagnoses accounted for 18% of admissions, so he made the (crude) assumption that depression therefore accounted for 18% of mental health care costs. Uprated to 1990 prices, this gave a value of £250 million. To this he added the price of general practitioner (GP) consultations for neurotic depression—3.5 million at £7.68 per consultation—giving £28 million at 1989 prices. Finally, the cash sales value of the antidepressant market was around £55 million in 1990. These figures thus gave him an overall total cost for treating depression of £333 million.

Although the methods we used were more detailed, the reasonably close agreement between his value and ours suggests that the figures are in roughly the right region.

The cost-effectiveness of pharmacological treatments for depression

The concept of cost-effectiveness implies a comparison, either between treatment and no treatment, or between different types of treatment. In view of the long history of reasonably successful pharmacological treatments of depression, it would be irrelevant and indeed unethical to compare a pharmacological treatment with no treatment. In our study, we compared two generations of antidepressant treatment: on the one hand, the tricyclic antidepressants represented by imipramine, and on the other, the new class of serotonin reuptake inhibitors, represented by paroxetine.

When used at full therapeutic doses, tricyclics are cheap and effective. Indeed, they are so effective that it would be difficult to demonstrate that a new competitor was more so, as it would require infeasibly large samples of patients. The new generation of antidepressants seem at any rate equally effective, but they do carry the disadvantage that they are relatively expensive. However, the tricyclic antidepressants have quite marked and troublesome side effects, whereas the latter antidepressants are relatively free of them. Although this is not immediately apparent, the level of side effects has an important bearing on cost-effectiveness.

There are three ways in which we might have obtained information about the cost and benefits of antidepressant treatment. An initial option, at first sight attractive, was for a comparative clinical trial that included economical evaluation. However, it was rejected, as a prospective clinical trial would take at least two years to report, but, more importantly, clinical trials do not accurately reflect routine clinical practice.

Another option was to observe the treatments prospectively in clinical practice: however, this too was rejected because it depended on the availability of marketed drugs and would also involve a large and long-term study.

We chose a third option. This involved developing a simulation model based on the theory of clinical decision analysis (Weinstein and Fineberg, 1980). It requires the construction of a decision tree to represent the logical and temporal sequencing of the clinical problem, and so provide a model of clinical practice.

In our model, the aim was to take whatever actions were required in order to obtain a successful outcome to treatment. The model is represented in Figure 2, and it requires some explanation. It takes the form of a branching tree. Each division represents a nodal point where outcome can differ. The initial nodal point is a choice point, being determined by the choice of one or other treatment. Once that decision has been made, subsequent decisions involves a response to circumstances, such as whether patients comply with treatment, whether they relapse, and so forth.

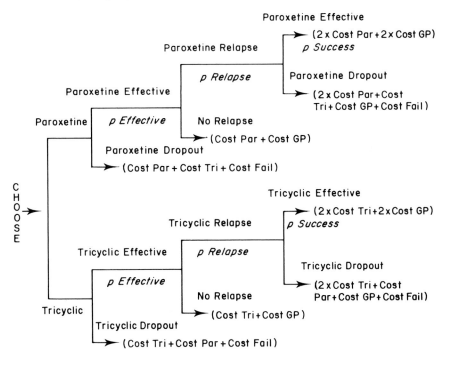

Figure 2. Model simulating clinical practice over 12 months.

It is assumed that the aim of the treating physician is to do whatever is necessary to obtain a successful outcome to treatment. In the course of treatment, individual patients take a unique course through the model. At each nodal point there is a probability that the patient will, as it were, go one way rather than the other. Each path through the model has specific costs associated with it. The average cost of using one or other of the two drugs in the comparison, is obtained by multiplying the costs implied by each of the possible paths by the probability that patients will take that particular path, then summing the values for 'cost × probability' separately for the paroxetine and imipramine sides of the model.

Thus, for example, if the first choice of treatment is successful, the costs involved comprise those of the course of treatment and of the GP's time. If the original choice of treatment was unsuccessful, we assumed there was a switch of drug (from imipramine to paroxetine, or vice versa). All treatment failures in our model thus incurred the cost of one course of imipramine and one course of paroxetine. Even after successful treatment, patients may relapse. We allowed for this possibility and assumed that patients who relapsed after initial successful treatment would receive another course of the same antidepressant. We counted patients who responded to a second course of the drug as successfully treated.

Our definition of *effective treatment* requires comment. We assumed that the effectiveness of treatment was calculated as 1 minus the dropout rate (1–D), i.e. the proportion of patients remaining on the drugs. We assumed that if patients did not drop out due to side effects or lack of effect, their treatment was successful. This is clearly an oversimplification, as there must be a proportion of people receiving the drug who fail to respond to it. However, available evidence suggests that failure to respond affects paroxetine and imipramine equally (Dunbar *et al.*, 1991) and thus can be omitted from the model.

We used data from different sources, in particular the results from phase III clinical trials, in order to calculate relative cost-effectiveness from the model. The data were assumed to cover a period of 12 months. We adopted a value for the dropout rate of 54% for imipramine and 42% for paroxetine; this was obtained from a pooled analysis of six randomized, double-blind, placebo-controlled studies carried out in the USA (Dunbar *et al.*, 1991). The analysis involved 726 patients treated for a period of six weeks. As this is one of the largest studies conducted with paroxetine, these data were considered to be more reliable than other available sources. The significantly greater dropout rate in imipramine-treated patients than paroxetine-treated patients is related to the side effect profile of the two drugs (see Table II).

Some of the data required for calculations based on the model were unavailable. We felt that the best way of obtaining reasonable estimates was to seek the opinions of clinicians selected for their known expertise in the management of depressed patients. We set up a panel of eight clinicians, consultant psychia-

Table II. Overview of reasons for dropout from intention-to-treat sample.

Reason for dropout	Paroxetine (n = 240) No. (%)	Placebo (n = 240) No. (%)	Imipramine (n = 237) No. (%)
Lack of efficacy	25 (10)[a]	79 (33)	17 (7) [c]
Adverse events	55 (23)[a,b]	21 (9)	85 (36)[c]
Other	22 (9)	28 (12)	25 (11)

[a] Fisher's exact test, paroxetine–placebo difference, $p \geq 0.001$.
[b] Fisher's exact test, paroxetine–imipramine difference, $p \geq 0.001$.
[c] Fisher's exact test, imipramine–placebo difference, $p \geq 0.001$.
Source: Dunbar *et al.* (1991). Reproduced with permission.

trists or GPs with a special interest in psychiatry. We sent a questionnaire to them, and then five of the panel met to review the results, to clarify the questions and answers, and produce a final report. Although the members of the panel had the opportunity to compare their answers and discuss similarities and differences, no attempt was made to achieve consensus: members of the panel gave their own answers. Results of this exercise were then presented to six psychiatrists, six hospital pharmacists, and three groups of eight GPs. These groups expressed no reservations over the panel results.

Values for daily treatment costs used in the model were £0.20 for imipramine and £1.13 for paroxetine. Our calculations of the costs of treating depression in general practice assumed that consultation for depression would involve 15 minutes of the GP's time. This is double the average British duration of a consultation with a general practitioner. We left the costs from suicide attempts out of the model because of the low incidence (1–2%).

The results of the expert panel (Table III) were combined with the unit cost data in Table I to give the cost associated with treatment failure (Figure 3). This value requires comment. It is apparent that the failure to treat depression effectively in the first instance adds very considerably to the overall cost of treatment: the consequences of treatment failure are very expensive indeed. As an example, although only 5% of treatment failure ends in hospital, hospitalization overall makes an appreciable contribution to overall costs. This accounts for the relatively small contribution to the overall cost of treatment of the cost of the tablets themselves.

McCombs and colleagues (1990) made estimates of the cost of treatment failure and depression. This was based on data from California Medicare programme in the period 1983–1988. Interestingly, they arrived at a figure of $1000, which is very close to our own figure of £488.00.

Our model revealed that the expected cost of treatment per patient was similar, irrespective of treatment outcome, namely £430 for paroxetine compared with £424 for imipramine. At first sight, this result runs counter to

Table III.   Results from the expert panel study.

Variable	Values used in model	Range of results given by panel
1. Average length of a primary course	12 weeks	8–12 weeks
2. GP visits?	6	5–6
3. Probability of relapse?	25%	20–30%
4. Patients successfully treated by further course?	60%	40–80%
5. Dropouts successfully treated?	60%	50–60%
6. Dropouts—inpatients?	5%	5–6%
7. Average length of stay	14 days	14–21 days
8. Attempt suicide?	—[a]	1–4%
9. Dropouts—visits to GP?	10	6–12
10. Dropouts—outpatients?	5	5–6
11. Dropouts—psychotherapy?	4%	2–4%
12. Sessions of psychotherapy?	6	5–6
13. Dropouts—ECT?	1%	—[b]
14. Sessions of ECT?	6	—[b]

[a] Not included in model.
[b] All panel members in agreement.

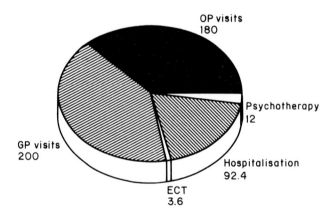

OP visits
180

Psychotherapy
12

GP visits
200

Hospitalisation
92.4

ECT
3.6

Total Cost: £488

Figure 3.   The cost of treatment failure (£).

intuition, given the five- to six-fold difference in price between the drugs. However, what imipramine gains from its low cost per tablet, paroxetine makes up, in virtue of its greater tolerability and lower dropout rate.

When we turn to the cost per *successfully treated* patient per year, paroxetine actually has an advantage. Thus the average cost per successfully treated patient for paroxetine was £785, while that for imipramine was £1024. This indicates that paroxetine was more cost-effective than conventional but less well-tolerated antidepressant therapy.

This result is obviously conditional on the values used in the model. Many of these values are best guesses, and it therefore seemed appropriate to undertake a sensitivity analysis. Clearly, if small changes in our chosen values make a considerable difference to the result, our conclusions must be viewed with scepticism. On the other hand, it is quite possible that the overall results are robust in the face of appreciable differences in individual values. Sensitivity analyses were conducted, whereby we examined the effect of choosing end-of-range values from our estimates rather than the mean. We were able to do this for the cost of treatment failure, the cost of GP visits, the probability of relapse, and the probability of successful treatment after relapse. The effects of these analyses are shown in Table IV. From this it can be seen that the similarities in the expected cost per patient treated were virtually unaffected by choosing end-of-range values. The most sensitive variable analysed was actually the cost of treatment failure. Using the highest value, paroxetine has a lower expected cost per patient, while using the lower value the expected cost per patient was still only 10% lower for imipramine.

The variable to which the results are crucially sensitive is the relative effectiveness of the drugs. Figure 4 shows how the mean cost per patient varies when the effectiveness of paroxetine is altered and that of imipramine is kept constant, while Figure 5 summarizes an equivalent analysis for the cost per successfully treated patient.

Table IV.   Sensitivity analysis.

	Values used in model		Expected cost per patient (£)	
			Imipramine	Paroxetine
Cost of treatment failure (£)	Main	488	430	424
	Low	300	314	340
	High	700	548	531
Cost of GP visit (£)	Main	120	430	424
	Low	60	392	390
	High	180	456	470
Probability of relapse	Main	25%	430	424
	Low	20%	416	419
	High	30%	431	441
Probability of successful treatment after relapse	Main	60%	430	424
	Low	50%	429	436
	High	75%	416	422

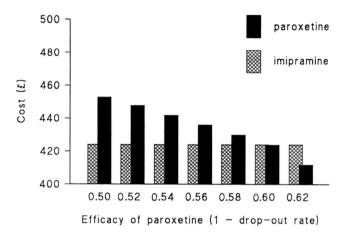

Figure 4.   Comparison of paroxetine and imipramine: cost per treated patient.

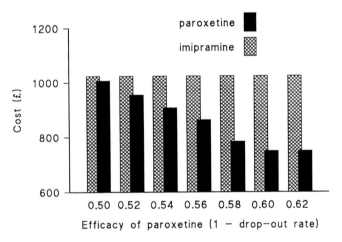

Figure 5.   Comparison of paroxetine and imipramine: cost per successfully treated patient.

Another measure of relevance to this sort of analysis is that of *marginal cost-effectiveness*. Marginal cost-effectiveness is the most useful measure for decisions about resource allocation: it provides an estimate of the price to be paid for the additional effectiveness of the most effective treatment.

The concept may be difficult for non-economists to grasp. It may be understood by using an analogy. If a firm has the option of buying a machine producing 100 units per day for £10 000, or one producing 120 for £14 000, the cost per unit produced of the first machine is £100, while that of the second is £116.70. The cost per *additional* unit is, however, £200. This is equivalent to

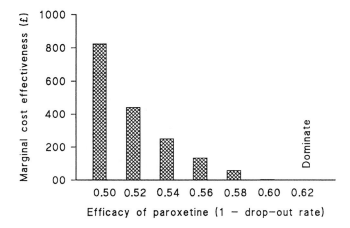

Figure 6.   Marginal cost effectiveness of paroxetine: relation to efficacy.

marginal cost-effectiveness, and allows the producer to decide if this is a reasonable price to pay for additional capacity. As the price of the second machine is brought down, the price for additional production falls, i.e. the marginal cost-effectiveness diminishes. If the more productive machine costs only £9999, it offers higher production at less cost. Translating this back into the language of our study, this is equivalent to the point at which a drug comes to offer better treatment at lower cost. The drug is then said to *dominate*.

Results for marginal cost-effectiveness are shown in Figure 6. It shows that the values for cost-effectiveness obtained in the clinical trials for paroxetine are such that the drug is close to giving better results at lower cost.

Our calculations to establish the cost-effectiveness of treatment with one of the new SSRIs naturally contain a number of assumptions. We have tried to show that the result is relatively insensitive to errors in our underlying estimates. The results do suggest that paroxetine is more cost-effective than conventional treatment with imipramine, as the cost per successfully treated patient was lower.

It could be argued that the apparent savings made with paroxetine are not real savings. In theory, if GPs spend less time treating depressive illness because they manage it more successfully, their time would become available for the treatment of other conditions. However, it cannot be guaranteed that the GP will not prefer to increase his or her leisure time instead. Thus the saving may be notional rather real.

Nevertheless, even if we take the most conservative view, the implication of our findings is that treatment with one of the new SSRIs should not be shunned because of prejudices about the cost per tablet. For the practising physician, this brings the reassurance that a humane choice of treatment is not soul-searchingly expensive.

References

American Psychiatric Association (1987) *Diagnostic and Statistical Manual of Mental Disorders*, 3rd edn, revised. Washington, DC: APA.

Bebbinton PE (1987) Marital status and depression: a study of English national admission statistics. *Acta Psychiatr. Scand* **75**, 640–650.

Bebbington PE (1992) The epidemiology of depressive illness. In: Montegomery S (ed.) *The Psychopharmacology of Depression*. BAP Monograph Services, Oxford: Oxford University Press.

Department of Health and Social Security and Office of Population Censuses and Surveys (1987) *Hospital Inpatient Inquiries, 1985*, main tables. Hospital Activity Analyses. Series MB4, No. 27. London: HMSO.

Dunbar GC, Cohn JB, Fabre LF *et al.* (1991) A comparison of paroxetine, imipramine and placebo in depressed outpatients. *Br J Psychiatry* **159**, 394–398.

Fadden GB, Bebbington PE and Kuipers L (1987a) The burden of care: the impact of functional psychiatric illness on the patient's family. *Br J Psychiatry* **150**, 285–292.

Fadden GB, Kuipers L and Bebbington PE (1987b) Caring and its burdens: a study of the relatives of depressed patients, *Br J Psychiatry* **151**, 660–667.

Health and Personal Social Statistics Report (1985) London: HMSO.

Hodgson TA and Meiners MR (1982) Cost-of-illness methodology: a guide to current practices and procedures. *Millbank Memorial Fund Quarterly/Health and Society* **60**, 429–491.

Hurry J, Bebbington PE and Tennant C (1987) Psychiatric symptoms and social disablement as determinants of illness behaviour. *Aust NZ J Psychiatry* **21**, 68–74.

McCombs JS, Nichol MB, Stimmel GL, *et al.* (1990) The cost of antidepressant drug therapy failure: a study of antidepressant use patterns in a Medicaid population. *J Clin Psychiatry* **51**, 60–69.

Paykel ES, Weissman MM, Prusoff BS (1978) Social maladjustment and severity of depression. *Compr Psychiatry* **19**, 121–128.

Prescription Pricing Authority/Department of Health (1988) *Prescription Cost Analysis System*. London: HMSO.

Royal College of General Practitioners (1986) *Morbidity Survey for General Practice. Third National Survey (1981–82)*. Series MB5, No. 1. London: HMSO.

Stoudemire A, Frank R, Hedemark N *et al* (1986) The economic burden of depression. *Gen Hosp Psychiatry* **8**, 387–394.

Weinstein MC, Fineberg HV (1980) *Clinical Decision Analysis*. Philadelphia: Saunders.

Weissman M, Prussoff B, Thompson W, Harding P and Myers J (1978) Social adjustment by self report in a community sample and in psychiatric out-patients. *J Nerv Mental Dis* **166**, 317–326.

West R (1992) *Depression*. London: Office of Health Economics.

World Health Organization (1978) *Mental Disorders: Glossary and Guide to their Classification in Accordance with the Ninth Revision of the International Classification of Diseases*. Geneva: WHO.

4

The cost of treatment failure

Jeffrey S. McCombs and Michael B. Nichol

Introduction

In this chapter, previously published data on the risk and cost of drug therapy failure for major depressive disorder (MDD) are reviewed. However, before presenting these data, it is instructive to discuss briefly how such risk and cost data have been developed and used by physicians in the past, and why more precise estimates are now being developed. Risk in this context is differentiated into the risk of adverse side effects and the risk of treatment failure. Costs are also differentiated into two parts: the direct cost of the health care resources required to treat adverse side effects and therapeutic failure, and the indirect costs from increased morbidity and mortality which are assumed primarily by the patient.

Drug utilization decisions have historically been the domain of the prescribing physicians. In selecting a medication, the physician balanced the expected benefits of alternative products against the risks and direct and indirect costs assumed by the patient. Physicians relied on their clinical experience, published data in the medical literature, and marketing materials provided by drug manufacturers to develop an assessment of the patterns of risks and benefits which applied to their patient population. The reliance on the individual physician to establish cost-effective drug treatment protocols is clearly inefficient and may also be ineffective. As a result the autonomy of the physician in prescribing is being challenged.

Clinical experience, the medical literature and marketing materials have significant limitations as sources of information on the risk of treatment failure,

Health Economics of Depression. Edited by B. Jönsson and J. Rosenbaum
© 1993 John Wiley & Sons Ltd.

particularly for depression. First, most depressed patients are treated initially by a primary care physician (Hohmann *et al.*, 1991). If depressed patients who fail drug therapy self-refer to a mental health specialist or simply withdraw from treatment, then the primary care physician may underestimate the failure rate of the prescribed drug therapy. Second, clinical trial literature for drugs used to treat mental disorders may significantly overestimate the drug's efficacy rate in real practice due to the intensity with which drug trial patients are monitored and encouraged to stay on the medication. Furthermore, drug trials last a short time relative to the time required to successfully treat mental disorders in clinical practice.

Reliable data on the direct and indirect costs of adverse side effects and treatment failure are even more difficult for the practising physician to develop individually or obtain from published literature. Even assuming that the physician is aware of the patient having failed drug therapy, the physician does not have complete data on the patient's use of health care services with which to estimate costs. Health economists and other researchers have also found that access to data on direct health care costs associated with treatment failure is difficult to obtain, to say nothing of obtaining data on the indirect costs of morbidity and mortality. Fortunately, the collection of data on the economics of alternative drug therapies is becoming more commonplace in clinical trial protocols. The reasons for these changes stem from the changing role of the individual physician in determining how prescription medications will be used.

Growth in insurance coverage for drugs, either through private insurance or government programmes, increases the likelihood that physicians and patients will become insensitive to price differentials between alternative products within a therapeutic class. This insensitivity could result in the over-use of newer, more expensive medications which may offer only marginal therapeutic advantages over established products. In response, insurance companies and government programmes attempt to control physician prescribing patterns through formularies, global budgets, drug use review (DUR) and other methods. Pharmacy and therapeutic (P&T) committees and government advisory boards have assumed a larger role in determining prescribing protocols and are demanding better data on the cost-effectiveness of new medications in determining formulary additions or DUR criteria. Key elements in the cost-effectiveness profile of a new medication are the rate at which patients fail to respond or tolerate older medications and the consequent costs.

This chapter reviews previously published data on the risk and direct cost of treatment failure for patients being treated with antidepressants (McCombs *et al.*, 1990). These estimates were developed using retrospective data. These results are presented both to provide estimates of the frequency and cost of treatment failure for patients receiving antidepressant therapy and to illustrate the complexity and limitations of using retrospective data for this purpose.

Data

Study population
Data for this analysis were derived from a retrospective data file consisting of all paid claims for a random 5% sample of patients in the California receiving health care services under the auspices of the state's Medicaid programme for the poor and disabled (Medi-Cal). The demographic characteristics of the Medi-Cal population vary significantly from the general population of California as illustrated in Figures 1–3. The Medi-Cal population is predominantly young, but also includes a larger proportion of elderly than the general population. Black and other non-white racial groups are over-represented, as are females.

Paid claims data for each Medi-Cal recipient in the sample were maintained for as long as the patient remained eligible for the programme. Each paid claim contained extensive information about the service received, including type of service, data of service, amount billed, amount paid and units (days) of service. Limited diagnostic information was available, primarily on hospital claims. Prescription drug claims included data identifying the specific product, strength and number of units dispensed and the date the prescription was filled.

Unit of analysis
These paid claims data were used to identify new patient episodes of antidepressant therapy. First, all Medi-Cal recipients filling a prescription for an antidepressant were identified and their full paid claims history retrieved (see Appendix A for the antidepressants included in the study). Next, the first

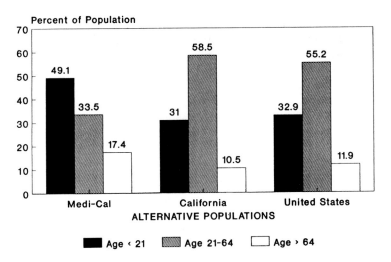

Figure 1.   Comparative age distributions: Medi-Cal/California/USA. (Data from the *Medicare and Medicaid Data Book*, 1988 and The *Statistical Abstract of the United States*, 1987.)

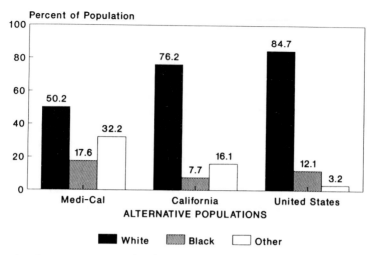

Figure 2.   Comparative race distributions: Medi-Cal/California/USA. (Data from the *Medicare and Medicaid Data Book*, 1988 and The *Statistical Abstract of the United States*, 1987.)

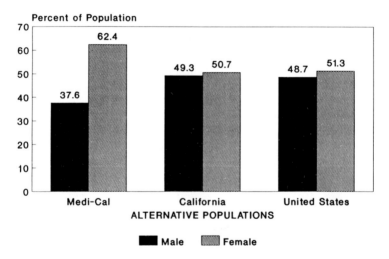

Figure 3.   Comparative gender distributions: Medi-Cal/California/USA. (Data from the *Medicare and Medicaid Data Book*, 1988 and The *Statistical Abstract of the United States*, 1987.)

antidepressant prescription on the patient's file was identified and its date of service used to partition the patient's stream of paid claims into a six-month pre-episode time period and a one-year post-episode period. New episodes of antidepressant therapy were identified by screening patients for a complete six months of eligibility prior to their first antidepressant prescription.

A total of 14 589 patients were identified as having used an antidepressant at some time during the study period (July 1983 to December 1987). However, only 6713 patients (46%) could be classified as having begun a new episode of antidepressant therapy. Clearly, a significant number of patients were either using antidepressants consistently throughout the study or the patient's stream of paid claims began about the time treatment is initiated. This latter case would be less of a problem in retrospective data retrieved from programmes in which eligibility for coverage is not dependent on income.

Estimation of direct treatment costs

The direct costs of services consumed in each period were estimated for the categories listed in Table I. An estimation procedure was required to fill in gaps in the paid claims data for Medi-Cal recipients who were also eligible for Medicare—the federally funded programme in the USA for the elderly and disabled. Medicare is the primary payer for most services for the dually eligible patient, while Medi-Cal payments for these patients were limited to the Medicare deductibles for ambulatory and hospital care, and to the Medicare 20% coinsurance on non-institutional services. These limitations mean that Medi-Cal data for patients 65 years of age or older understated the total direct cost incurred. While epidemiological data suggest that depression is less prevalent in the elderly (Regier *et al.*, 1984), the elderly represent a significant proportion of the population eligible for Medi-Cal.

In order to fill these gaps in data, the analysis converted data for days of hospital and skilled nursing facility (SNF) care into an estimate of total direct cost for these services only for patients over 65 years of age at the time of the initial antidepressant prescription. Hospital days are assumed to cost society $643 per day, while SNF days are assumed to cost $60 per day. These per diem costs approximate the average cost for these services to Medi-Cal and Medicare, respectively (California's Medical Assistance Program, 1988; Latta and Keene, 1989). An estimate of the cost of ambulatory services was not attempted, which will result in an underestimation of any ambulatory costs associated with treatment failure. Direct costs for patients under 65 years of age used the actual amount paid by Medi-Cal as recorded on each paid claim.

Table I.   Categories of services for study.

Physicians' (psychiatric)	Physicians' (non-psychiatric)
Psychologist	Lab and X-ray
Prescription drugs	Dental services
Intermediate care facility	Skilled nursing facility
Hospital services (acute)	Hospital services (extended)
Hospital services (rehab.)	State hospital services
Hospital outpatients	Other outpatient clinics
All other services	

Failure rates and the cost of treatment failure

Identifying patients and measuring outcomes

Mental illness diagnoses may be under-reported on paid claims data due to social stigma or other factors. This was found to be the case in the Medi-Cal data. As an alternative, patients with major depressive disorder (MDD) were identified and their treatment outcomes classified depending on the dose and duration of their antidepressant regimen and upon the utilization of other psychoactive medications. The identification of MDD patients was complicated by the fact that antidepressants were used to treat other psychological disorders such as anxiety, neurotic depression and adjustment disorders with depressed mood. Furthermore, the pharmacological properties of antidepressants are used to treat other non-psychiatric problems, such as chronic pain (Walsh, 1983).

The first step in the patient classification process was to specify a maximum 'non-MDD' dose for those antidepressants with other therapeutic applications. Patients who never achieved a dose above the maximum non-MDD dose (e.g. above 50 mg per day for amitriptyline) were assumed to be non-MDD patients and were excluded from further analysis. Not surprisingly, 2266 new patient episodes (33.8% of all new episodes) were excluded based on this dosing criteria. Data from the 1985 National Ambulatory Medical Care Survey indicated that 46% of prescriptions for tricyclic antidepressants written by family physicians are for non-psychiatric conditions. The corresponding data for general practitioners and internists are 60% and 48%, respectively (Broadhead *et al.*, 1991). In our Medi-Cal sample, some portion of the excluded patient category might represent improperly managed (underdosed) MDD patients, but it was not possible to estimate their number. However, data presented in the original study indicate that the nursing home cost per patient in this excluded population was nearly 70% higher than for patients used in the analysis. This result suggests that California physicians commonly prescribe low doses of antidepressants for poor, elderly patients in nursing homes.

Three additional patient groups were identified as being likely to be *complicated* MDD patients and were also excluded from the analysis: (1) patients who received concurrent prescriptions for an antipsychotic medication at the beginning of the antidepressant treatment episode ($n = 737$); (2) patients who received a concurrent, augmenting prescription for lithium within 30 days of the initial antidepressant prescription which was assumed indicative of bipolar or other complicated depressions ($n = 31$); and (3) patients who used some form of augmentation drug therapy (e.g. triiodothyronine T_3 or methylphenidate) within 30 days of the initial antidepressant prescription, including the concurrent use of two antidepressants ($n = 15$). The health care cost profiles of these depressed patient populations were expected to be radically different from those experienced by uncomplicated MDD patients.

The resulting 3664 new patient episodes of antidepressant therapy included at least one prescription above the non-MDD dose. These episodes were then screened for a minimum of 12 months of post-episode data. This final paring of the study population resulted in 2344 new patient episodes of antidepressant therapy to be further classified according to treatment outcome.

Antidepressant treatment success was defined based on consistent and persistent dosing of the patient above a predetermined minimum therapeutic dose set for each product studied. This minimum therapeutic dose exceeded the maximum non-MDD dose level discussed above which created a range of uncertain dosing. For example, the minimum therapeutic dose for amitriptyline was set at 75 mg per day compared to its maximum non-MDD dose of 50 mg per day. The consumption of an antidepressant prescription with an 'uncertain' dose may indicate sub-therapeutic dosing by the physician or patient non-compliance. Provisions were made in the outcome classification schema for a period of titration to the minimum therapeutic dose, for a change to a second antidepressant early in the episode of care, and for possible alternations between sequences of therapeutic and sub-therapeutic prescriptions.

A precise definition of 'persistent' was made difficult by the episodic nature of MDD, which is cyclical and may vary in duration (Gold *et al.*, 1988). Successful antidepressant therapy for MDD cannot be defined based simply on continuous use since episodic therapy may be appropriate. Conversely, any standard regarding a minimum length of therapy introduces imprecision and additional uncertainty into the determination of outcome. In this analysis, a successful MDD treatment episode was defined based on a consistent therapeutic dose maintained continuously for 180 days inclusive of a titration period not to exceed 45 days. However, not all successfully treated MDD patients meet this 'gold standard' of success. The following patients are also classified as MDD successes: (1) patients achieving the 'gold standard' after switching to a second antidepressant within 30 days of their initial prescription; (2) patients who end the titration period at a sub-therapeutic dose, continue therapy, and eventually achieve a consistent therapeutic dose as of the end of 180 days; and (3) patients who persist with therapy after an initial period of low doses and temporary discontinuations (<45 days) and achieve a consistent therapeutic dose for a minimum of 180 days.

Five types of prescription profiles were assumed to be clearly indicative of antidepressant treatment failure: (1) patients who switched between three or more antidepressants during the episode; (2) patients who began drug therapies designed to augment antidepressant efficacy after 30 days from the initial prescription, including the concurrent use of two antidepressants; (3) patients restarted therapy after a break in service in excess of 45 days; (4) patients who exhibited dosing levels which alternate between therapeutic and sub-therapeutic classifications; and (5) patients who had a recorded diagnosis of affective psychoses and who never achieve a consistent therapeutic dose.

Only 377 new patient episodes of an antidepressant drug therapy could be clearly classified as either a treatment success or treatment failure out of the

2344 patient episodes, which included at least one prescription above the maximum non-MDD dose (16.1%). Of these 377 patients, only 81 met the criteria for treatment success. This success rate (21.5%) is remarkably similar to results from a study at Group Health Cooperative of Puget Sound, which found that only 24% of distressed, high utilizers of primary care judged to require antidepressant therapy received an adequate course of drug therapy (Katon *et al.*, 1992). Both results are far below the 65–80% success rates reported in the clinical trial literature (Hirschfeld *et al.*, 1988; Baldessarini, 1989). Published success rates often report the proportion of compliant patients who achieve a satisfactory clinical response rather than the proportion of total patients achieving success. However, many clinical trials of antidepressant drugs do provide the data required to make these calculations. For example, John Feighner reported that only 10 of 22 (45%) amitriptyline patients continued with drug therapy beyond five weeks in a clinical comparison with fluoxetine (Feighner, 1985).

Nearly 30% of Medi-Cal patients never achieved an average daily dose above the specified minimum therapeutic dose for MDD for any of their sequences of antidepressant prescriptions. Approximately 60% of this category of patients discontinued therapy after only one or two sub-therapeutic prescriptions. This 'sub-therapeutic' classification of patients was likely to include non-MDD patients being treated with antidepressants for other problems, MDD treatment failures and, possibly, a few MDD treatment successes. The MDD treatment failures who discontinue therapy early are likely to have experienced significant difficulty with side effects. The MDD treatment failures with extended sub-therapeutic prescription profiles may include patients who are being under-dosed by their physician due to the complexities of effective antidepressant therapy, or patients who are non-compliant primarily to avoid side effects.

The majority of patients (54%) could not be classified into the success, failure or sub-therapeutic categories. These 'uncertain outcome' patients consumed at least one prescription above the minimum therapeutic dose for MDD specified for the product they were using, but did not maintain therapy at this dose for sufficient time to be classified as an MDD success. Likewise, their use of other augmenting therapies or alternative antidepressants was such that they cannot be clearly classified as MDD failures. Patients in this category typically discontinued therapy prior to the end of 180 days. Although the dose achieved on at least one prescription was suggestive of an MDD diagnosis, the longitudinal course of therapy suggested either an alternative diagnosis, an atypically short course of successful MDD therapy, or an MDD treatment failure.

In summary, the distribution of outcomes for new antidepressant episodes in the Medi-Cal programme indicates that the majority of patients were either not using antidepressants to treat depression or were not effectively treated for depression. The twin problems of mis-diagnoses and poor management of depressed patients in primary medical practice is both well documented and difficult to rectify (Eisenberg, 1992). The high failure rate for the drugs under study here suggests that the aggregate cost of MDD treatment failure could be substantial if the cost per treatment failure is found to be significant.

The cost of treatment failure

Table II presents data on the pre-episode and post-episode costs per month for the four outcome classifications of potential MDD patients who have a full 12 months of post-episode data. These data indicate that MDD treatment failure was costly in terms of post-episode medical care use. Only the MDD failure population experienced a significant increase in spending per month between the prior and post periods, increasing 18.3% compared to 0.9% for MDD successes. When the costs of prescription drugs were factored out, MDD successes experienced a decrease of 20% in net total costs while MDD failures experienced a 9.6% increase in net costs. But more importantly, expenditures for long-term care and acute hospital care increased significantly in the failure population while they remain constant or decrease for MDD successes. Average costs per patient-month was relatively stable for sub-therapeutic patients (−2.8%) and the uncertain patient population (4.6%). These changes in health care costs per patient-month for successes and failures are illustrated in Figure 4.

The incremental impact on health care costs of MDD treatment failure was estimated using multivariate regression analysis to control for patient age, sex and prior use of services. These results provide a more definitive picture of the effect of MDD treatment failure by type of service and by time period. In the regression model, treatment failures, sub-therapeutic patients and patients in

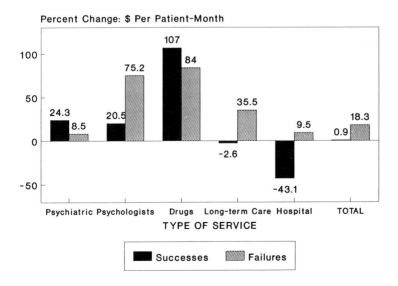

Figure 4.   The Medi-Cal antidepressant study. Percentage change: pre- to post-episode.

Table II.   Average monthly health care costs by type of service: pre-episode versus post-episode costs by outcome classification.

Cost category	Successes N = 81	Sub-therapeutic N = 698	Uncertain N = 1269	Failures N = 296
Prior use of care ($ per month)				
Psychiatric	6.63	1.84	2.20	11.97
Other physician	36.77	32.07	28.52	35.55
Psychologists	1.32	0.56	0.60	1.09
Lab and X-ray	3.90	3.32	2.75	4.26
Drugs	41.74	27.71	31.63	31.00
Dental	3.27	4.37	3.90	4.38
Long-term care	67.41	99.32	51.10	51.20
Hospital	70.37	84.55	89.91	102.21
OPD/clinics	22.41	16.14	16.39	23.35
Total (net drugs)	212.08	242.17	195.37	234.01
Total	253.82	269.88	227.00	265.01
Post-episode use of care ($ per month)				
Psychiatric	8.24	1.37	1.95	12.99
Other physician	26.18	29.10	27.80	32.79
Psychologists	1.59	0 61	0.57	1.91
Lab and X-ray	2.20	3.11	2.97	4.05
Drugs	86.42	41.11	49.72	57.04
Dental	6.19	3.75	3.69	4.43
Long-term care	65.68	103.58	69.31	69.36
Hospital	40.05	65.30	65.97	111.92
OPD/clinics	19.63	14.44	15.50	19.06
Total (net drugs)	169.76	221.26	187.76	256.51
Total	256.18	262.37	237.48	313.55
Percentage change (post-pre/pre)				
Psychiatric	24.3	−25.5	−11.4	8.5
Other physician	−28.8	−9.3	−2.5	−7.8
Psychologists	20.5	8.9	−5.0	75.4
Lab and X-ray	−43.6	−6.3	8.0	−4.9
Drugs	107.0	48.4	57.2	84.0
Dental	89.3	−14.2	−5.4	1.1
Long-term care	−2.6	4.3	35.6	35.5
Hospital	−43.1	−22.6	−26.6	9.5
OPD/clinics	−12.4	−10.5	−5.4	−18.4
Total (net drugs)	−20.0	−8.6	−3.9	9.6
Total	0.9	−2.8	4.6	18.3

the uncertain category were compared with the treatment successes. The multivariate analysis of the incremental cost of MDD treatment failure was based on the estimation of the following equation:

$$TC = \alpha + \beta_1 \text{ AGE} + \beta_2 \text{ SEX} + \Sigma_i \beta_i \text{ PRIOR}_i + \beta_3 \text{ FAIL} + \beta_4 \text{ UNCERTAIN} + \beta_5 \text{ SUB-THERAPEUTIC} + \varepsilon$$

where TC is the total cost of treating the MDD patient after the onset of the MDD episode as indicated by the antidepressant prescription; AGE is the patient's age

Table III. Estimated regression model of total cost net of drug costs: one year post-episode.

Independent level variable	Parameter estimate	t-statistic	Significance
		N = 2344	
Intercept	−970.83	−1.738	0.0823
Age (in months)	2.99	7.280	0.0001
Sex (1 = female)	−390.57	−1.887	0.0593
Failure	1265.65	2.329	0.0168
Uncertain	341.48	0.706	0.4805
Sub-therapeutic	226.27	0.456	0.6484
Use of services ($ six months prior)			
Psychiatric	0.16	0.180	0.8573
Other psysicians	0.94	3.332	0.0009
Psychologist	−0.53	−0.183	0.8551
Lab and X-ray	0.96	0.666	0.5056
Prescription drugs	1.34	3.700	0.0002
Dental	0.07	0.068	0.9460
ICF	2.17	10.660	0.0001
SNF	1.85	37.622	0.0001
Hospital	0.10	2.785	0.0054
Hospital, rehabilitation	−7.51	−0.715	0.4746
State mental hospital	1.33	0.159	0.8736
Hospital OPD	1.25	2.872	0.0041
Other clinics	0.74	0.247	0.8048
All other services	0.07	2.165	0.0305

Adjusted R^2 = 0.4476.
F-statistic = 100.921.

in months at the time of the initial antidepressant prescription; SEX = 1 if female; $PRIOR_i$ is a vector of expenditures during the six months prior to the MDD episode for the ith type of service; FAIL = 1 if the patient is classified as an MDD treatment failure; UNCERTAIN = 1 if the patient is classified in the uncertain category; and SUB-THERAPEUTIC = 1 if the patient never achieves a therapeutic dose.

The regression coefficient β_3 estimated the difference in cost associated with the patient failing antidepressant therapy *relative to MDD treatment successes*. Likewise, β_4 and β_5 measured the incremental cost differences between the uncertain and sub-therapeutic categories and treatment successes. Separate equations were estimated by type of service and for total direct costs. The hypothesis that treatment failure results in a significant increase in costs was tested using the significance levels for β_3 in each of the estimated equations.

The results of the multiple regression analysis of total direct costs minus drug costs are reported in Table III. These results indicate that MDD treatment failure was associated with an increase in direct costs of $1266 in the first year after the beginning of the episode of care ($p<0.02$). Age was positively correlated to costs ($2.99 per month of age, $p<0.0001$), while females experienced significantly lower costs (–$390.57, $p<0.06$). The prior use of non-psychiatric physicians' services, prescription drugs, intermediate care facility (ICF) and SNF services, hospital care and hospital outpatient department (OPD) care were all positively correlated with post-episode costs. Patients categorized either as uncertain or sub-therapeutic did not differ significantly from MDD successes in terms of total direct costs (+$342, $p<0.48$ and +$226, $p<0.65$, respectively). The total direct cost equation explains a large proportion of the total variance in per capita costs ($R^2=0.4476$).

The estimated direct cost of MDD treatment failure by type of service for Medi-Cal costs are summarized in Table IV. These results indicate that the additional direct costs associated with MDD treatment failure were due primarily to increased hospital costs ($921, $p<0.04$) which were offset partially by lower prescription drug costs (–$222, $p<0.001$). The effect of treatment failure on total direct cost was estimated to be $1043 ($p<0.06$).

Table IV. The estimated difference in episode costs by patient category: failure, uncertain and sub-therapeutic populations compared to the treatment success population.

| Characteristic | One year post-episode start $N = 2344$ | | | |
	Sub-therapeutic $N = 689$	Uncertain $N = 1269$	Failures $N = 298$	Adj. R^2
Type of service				
Psychiatric	−52.19***	−46.42***	25.62	0.4145
Other physician	99.17	103.95[a]	86.61	0.2747
Psychologists	−6.24	−6.97	7.25	0.4606
Lab and X-ray	19.22[a]	21.33*	19.55[a]	0.3792
Drugs	−385.19***	−331.52***	−221.83***	0.4505
Dental	−27.86*	−28.22*	−20.95	0.0069
ICF	3.19	18.00	10.86	0.8463
SNF	7.71	119.54	227.00	0.7594
Hospital	213.09	179.69	921.06*	0.0416
State hospital	0.70	0.84	−0.25	0.0132
OPD/clinics	−24.02	−12.50	−9.74	0.1972
Net (one year, no drugs)	226.27	341.48	1265.65*	0.4467
Total (one year)	−159.51	10.51	1042.63[a]	0.4564

[a] Statistically significant at $p < 0.10$.
* Statistically significant at $p < 0.05$.
** Statistically significant at $p < 0.01$.
*** Statistically significant at $p < 0.001$.

Source: McCombs *et al.* (1990). Reproduced with permission from *The Journal of Clinical Psychiatry*, **51**, (6, suppl.), 60–69. Copyright 1990, Physicians Postgraduate Press.

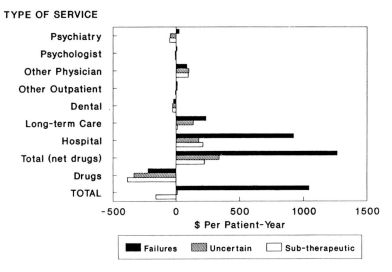

Figure 5.   The Medi-Cal antidepressant study. Comparison of estimated figures.

The difference in costs for the uncertain and sub-therapeutic patient categories relative to MDD treatment successes is also reported in Table IV. Both patient categories utilize significantly fewer psychiatric services and prescription drug costs than MDD treatment successes. These results are consistent with the hypothesis that these categories of patients included a significant proportion of non-MDD patients. The magnitude of the estimate effects of therapeutic failure relative to the estimated effects for the uncertain and sub-therapeutic populations are illustrated in Figure 5.

Conclusions

The results reported in McCombs *et al.* (1990) documented the patterns of antidepressant use by the California Medicaid population receiving treatment primarily from community-based physicians. The results indicate that as many as two-thirds of all patients using antidepressants were under treatment for problems other than depression or were being dosed sub-optimally.

While the data and methodology used to classify patients were imprecise, the magnitude to the population receiving sub-therapeutic doses or abbreviated courses of antidepressant therapy cannot be ignored. But more importantly, while existing antidepressant efficacy studies have reported an MDD treatment success rate of 65–80%, the success rate found in the Medi-Cal population for routine community practice falls well short of this level. At best, only 20–25% of MDD patients achieved a consistent, minimum therapeutic dose over a treatment period of approximately six months. The actual MDD success rate could be significantly below this level, possibly below 10% if all of the MDD treatment failures could be identified and counted. These results suggest that the standard antidepressants were either not particularly effective, were not being tolerated at recognized therapeutic doses for customary lengths of therapy, or were not being used correctly by community-based physicians.

Treatment failure for MDD patients was estimated to cost approximately $1000 in additional health care services during the first year after the start of antidepressant therapy. The majority of these costs accrued in the first six months and were concentrated in hospital inpatient services. The increased cost associated with MDD treatment failure included the reduction in prescription drug costs of $222 due to patient withdrawal from drug therapy.

These results suggest that new, effective antidepressants may find ready acceptance into the physicians' drug therapy arsenal. The high costs associated with treatment failure suggest that third-party payers may benefit from reduced programme costs if the new antidepressants now entering the market can improve the MDD treatment success rate. These newer products may be particularly useful if they exhibit a more benign side effect profile, thus simplifying the management of MDD patients by community-based physicians.

References

Baldessarini RJ (1989) Current status of antidepressants: clinical pharmacology and therapy. *J Clin Psychiatry* **50**, 117–126.

Broadhead WE, Larson DB, Yarnall KSH, Blazer DG and Tse CJ (1991) Tricyclic antidepressant prescribing for nonpsychiatric disorders. *J Fam Pract* **33**, 24–32.

California's Medical Assistance Program (1988) Annual statistical report, calendar year 1987, State of California, Department of Health Services, Medical Care Statistics Section, Sacramento, CA.

Eisenberg L (1992) Treating Depression and Anxiety in primary care. *N Engl J Med* **376**(16), 1080–84.

Feighner JP (1985) A comparative trial of fluoxetine and amitriptyline in patients with major depressive disorder. *J Clin Psychiatry* **46**, 369–372.

Gold PW, Goodwin FK and Chrousos GP (1988) Clinical and biochemical manifestations of depression: relation to the neurobiology of stress. *N Engl J Med* **319**, 348–353.

Health Care Financing Administration (1988) Program statistics: *Medicare and Medicaid Data Book.* HCFA publication no. 03270. Baltimore: Department of Health and Human Services.

Hirschfeld RMA and Goodwin FK (1988) Mood disorders. In: Talbott JA, Hales RE and Yudofsky SC (eds.) *Textbook of Psychiatry*, pp. 403–441. Washington, DC: American Psychiatric Press.

Hohmann AA, Larson DB, Thompson JW, Beardsley RS (1991) Psychotropic medication prescription in US ambulatory medical care. *DICP Ann Pharmachother* **25**, 85–89.

Kayton W, Von Korff M, Lin E, Bush T and Ormel J (1992) Adequacy and duration of antidepressant treatment in primary care. *Med Care* **30**, 67–76.

Latta VB and Keene RE (1989) Use and cost of skilled nursing facility services under Medicare. *Health Care Financing Rev* **11**, 105–112.

McCombs JS, Nichol MB, Stimmel GL *et al.* (1990) The cost of antidepressant drug therapy failure: a study of antidepressant use patterns in a Medicaid population. *J Clin Psychiatry* **51** (suppl.), 60–69.

Regier DA, Myers JK, Kramer M *et al.* (1984) The NIMH epidemiological catchment area program. *Arch Gen Psychiatry* **41**, 934–941.

Statistical Abstract of the United States (1987) US Department of Commerce, Bureau of the Census, Washington DC.

Walsh TD (1983) Antidepressants in chronic pain. *Clin Neuropharmacol* **6**, 271–295.

Appendix A: antidepressants for study

Drug	Non-MDD dose (mg)	Minimum therapeutic dose (mg)
Amitriptyline	50	75
Imipramine	50	75
Desipramine	50	75
Protriptyline	10	20
Nortriptyline	25	50
Trazodone	100	150
Doxepin	50	75
Maprotiline	50	75
Amoxapine	100	150
Phenelzine (Nardil)	n.a.	45
Tranylcypromine (Parnate)	n.a.	20
Isocarboxazid (Marplan)	n.a.	10

Augmentation medications

Lithium
Triiodothyronine (T$_3$)
Amphetamine
Methylphenidate (Ritalin)

Antipsychotic medications (neuroleptics)

Chlorpromazine (Thorazine)
Thioridazine (Mellaril)
Trifluoperazine (Stelazine)
Fluphenazine (Prolixin)
Perphenazine (Trilafon)
Thiothixene (Navane)
Molindone (Moban)
Loxapine (Loxitane)
Haloperidol (Haldol)

5

The financial implications of starting treatment with a selective serotonin reuptake inhibitor or tricyclic antidepressant in drug-naive depressed patients

William F. Boyer and John P. Feighner

Introduction

Over the past few years several selective serotonin reuptake inhibitors (SSRIs) have been introduced in the USA and other countries. They have become successful largely because they are much better tolerated than previous generations of antidepressants, especially the tricyclic antidepressants (TCAs). However, they are more expensive than earlier antidepressants, most of which are available in generic form. This expense has been a hindrance to their acceptance in some situations, such as managed care programmes where pharmacy costs are closely scrutinized. This chapter will examine in more detail the cost differences between choosing an SSRI or TCA for first-line treatment of depression. This presumes that the patient has no history of previous treatment for depression, since a history of response or non-tolerance of a particular agent should influence treatment choice. For example, if a patient had previously responded well to an SSRI or TCA it would be bad practice to start them on another agent. If they had poorly tolerated a certain drug clinicians should be less likely to start with a drug from the same class.

A study by Johnson in 1981 emphasized the need for better-tolerated

Health Economics of Depression. Edited by B. Jönsson and J. Rosenbaum
© 1993 John Wiley & Sons Ltd.

antidepressants (Johnson, 1981). In this study 92% of depressed patients who attended a general practitioner in Sweden were treated with TCAs, the remainder with minor tranquillizers. Fully 68% of patients stopped their medication within four weeks, 36% of whom did so because of side effects. This leaves a compliance rate of only 32%. Sedation and dry mouth, the hallmarks of TCA therapy, were the most poorly tolerated. More recent data from a large health maintenance organization showed that only 20% of patients receiving prescriptions for first-generation antidepressants, such as amitriptyline or imipramine, filled four or more prescriptions. This is similar to the 32% figure in the Johnson study. It also suggests that few patients prescribed these drugs receive adequate treatment for an episode of clinical depression (Katon et al., 1992).

Table I illustrates the retail costs of SSRIs and several TCAs in a large pharmacy chain in southern California. It also illustrates the projected medication cost for a six-month course of treatment. Costs were checked at other large retail pharmacies and found to be almost identical.

Table I shows that the retail cost per patient for six months' treatment with SSRIs compares favourably with the cost of proprietary tertiary and secondary amine TCAs and the generic secondary amine compounds. The popularity of

Table I.   Retail costs of SSRIs and TCAs.

	Dosage form (mg)	Therapeutic dose range (mg per day)	Price per 100 (US $)	Retail drug cost per six-month episode (US $)	
				low	high
SSRIs					
Fluoxetine	20	20–80	181.97	327.55	1310.18
Paroxetine	20	20–50	169.00	304.20[a]	—
	30		323.88	—	887.18[b]
Sertraline	50	50–200	175.95	316.71	1266.8[d]
	100		181.96	163.76[c]	655.06[d]
TCAs					
Tertiary amine					
Amitriptyline	50, generic	150–300	8.53	46.06	92.12
	50, proprietary	150–300	73.95	399.33	798.66
Imipramine	50, generic	150–300	9.97	53.84	107.68
	50, proprietary	150–300	70.81	382.37	764.75
Secondary amine					
Nortriptyline	25, generic	50–150	58.02	313.31	626.62
	25, proprietary	50–150	77.36	417.74	835.49
Desipramine	50, generic	150–300	37.98	205.09	410.18
	50, proprietary	150–300	93.57	505.28	1010.56

Prices per large southern Californian retail pharmacy chain.
[a] 20 mg daily.
[b] 20 mg + 30 mg daily.
[c] One half of a 100 mg tablet.
[d] Two 100 mg tablets.

the SSRIs actually helps control their retail cost. For pharmacies to remain competitive they accept a lower margin of profit for large-volume items such as these. Because TCAs are less popular there is less competition and more price variability.

If one assumes that patients will be treated with an average of 150 mg per day of a TCA or, for the SSRIs, 20 mg per day of fluoxetine or paroxetine or 50–100 mg per day of sertraline, the cost of SSRI treatment is actually less than the cost of proprietary TCAs. The cost is comparable to treatment with the generic secondary amine TCAs nortriptyline and desipramine. The cost of treatment with 50 mg of sertraline per day taken as one half of the 100 mg tablet is less than all but the generic tertiary amine TCAs amitriptyline and imipramine. However, a number of patients will require more than 50 mg per day.

Table I shows that the largest cost difference is between the SSRIs and generic tertiary amine TCAs such as amitriptyline and imipramine. However, the tertiary amine TCAs have more significant side effects than their secondary amine cousins and therefore are often not used for first-line treatment (Settle, 1992; Roose *et al.*, 1987; McCue, 1992; Jenike, 1989; Seppala and Linnoila, 1983; Blackwell *et al.*, 1980). Whether generic compounds are as fully effective and as well tolerated as the proprietary brand is also questionable. Nevertheless the cost comparison model presented in this chapter will compare the price of the average of generic amitriptyline, imipramine, nortriptyline and desipramine to treatment with fluoxetine (20 mg per day) or sertraline (100 mg per day taken as a single 100 mg tablet). The null hypothesis will be that treatment with generic TCAs is much less expensive than SSRI treatment.

Building the model

The primary clinical difference between TCAs and SSRIs is that the latter are much better tolerated by the average patient. This will form the basis of the cost comparison. As will be seen, most of the cost differences come from patients who do not tolerate or respond to treatment. Collectively these will be termed the first-line treatment failures.

Data taken from seven antidepressant drug trials at the Feighner Research Institute (total $N=636$) will form the basis of our estimates. These trials were controlled comparisons of an SSRI (fluoxetine, paroxetine or fluvoxamine) with a TCA (imipramine, amitriptyline or doxepin) and/or placebo. The data are presented in Table II.

Response was defined as a six-week Clinical Global Impressions Improvement (CGI) score of 1 or 2, which corresponds to 'moderate' or 'marked' improvement. Some of the patients who dropped out of active drug treatment were also responders (25%). Their improvement was presumably unrelated to medication. We will use 25% in our model as an estimate of the proportion of

Table II.   Clinical results in seven antidepressant drug trials (Feighner Research Institute).

	TCAc (N = 156)	SSRIs (N = 261)
Non-compliers (dropouts)	52%	42%
Responders (percentage of completers)	63%	70%

patients who drop out of treatment but do not require further therapy. It is interesting that this 25% figure resembles the response rate of placebo-treated patients (33%) in these same studies.

There are several financial risks inherent in first-line treatment failure. These patients will, on average, be seen more often by their treating physicians, are more likely to be referred to specialists and may have more diagnostic tests performed. A percentage of these patients will also require psychiatric hospitalization.

Table III estimates the total direct costs of treatment with TCAs or SSRIs over a six-month period. We assume that 1000 patients start treatment with either a TCA or SSRI. Other assumptions are listed and referenced in the table. The table shows that while medication costs are less with TCAs, if one adds the costs of hospitalization and outpatient visits it would cost an average of $47 257 per 1000 or $47 more per patient to start treatment with a TCA than with an SSRI.

Table III.   Anticipated costs for six months' treatment (1000 patients starting in each drug group).

Source	Difference in costs (SSRIs–TCAs)
Hospitalization	–$67 188
Outpatient visits	–$11 546
Medication	+$31 476
Total	–$47 257

Assumptions		Reference
Cost of TCAs/week	$5.95	Table I
Cost of SSRIs/week	$12.39	Table I
Hospitalization cost	$7635	Bentkover *et al.* (1992)
Hospitalization rate	11%	Bentkover *et al.* (1992)
Outpatient visits		
First-line successes	12	Bentkover *et al.* (1992)
Extra for failures	3.5	Bentkover *et al.* (1992)
Cost per visit	$119	Bentkover *et al.* (1992)

SSRI failures are switched to TCAs and TCA failures are switched to SSRIs

The magnitude of the cost difference in the medication category may seem small compared to the difference in costs between SSRIs and TCAs. However, this cost projection concerns the implications of which medicine is prescribed first. Therefore if a patient is started on a TCA and later is switched to an SSRI, the SSRI cost goes into the TCA category. It is also worth emphasizing that the estimated hospitalization rate of 11% is for patients who fail or drop out of first-line treatment. The hospitalization rate for depressed patients before or during their first course of treatment is probably lower. The model also assumes that the patients who fail TCAs are switched to SSRIs and vice versa.

Testing the model

Since this model utilized a number of estimates it is important to test them. It appears from Table III that the largest source of the cost difference between SSRIs and TCAs is due to psychiatric hospitalization. This is similar to the findings of McCombs and colleagues (1990), who reported that treatment failure in major depressive disorder was associated with a significant increase in costs, much of which was due to psychiatric hospitalization.

Smaller TCA–SSRI cost differences occur in this model with lower hospitalization rates. However, starting a patient on a TCA is more expensive with hospitalization rates down to 3%. If one assumes higher costs of hospitalization than the $7635 used in the model, SSRIs become even more economical.

Some basic health care plans do not provide inpatient psychiatric benefits. This would translate to a hospitalization rate of 0%. With a 0% hospitalization rate the model predicts that starting patients on a TCA would save $10–$19 per patient. However, even this small amount is probably too high since patients who are ill enough to require hospitalization are almost certain to require a greater amount of outpatient resources if they cannot be hospitalized.

The data collected at the Feighner Research Institute suggest that the 11% estimated hospitalization rate used in the model is reasonable. The patients who are most likely to be hospitalized after failing treatment are those who get worse or do not improve. In our data 9.5% of patients on active drug were rated worse on the CGI at the end of their study, and an additional 18% were no better.

The cost of office visits and the estimated numbers of visits for first-line treatment responders, non-responders and dropouts were also tested. TCAs remain more expensive than SSRIs even if the cost of office visits is set at zero. Smaller TCA–SSRI cost differences occur with more visits for first-line treatment responders. However, there would have to be 29 first-line visits for the cost of TCAs to equal SSRIs. There are no numbers of visits for first-line treatment failures or dropout improvers at which starting treatment with TCAs is less expensive.

It might be possible for some organizations to provide TCAs at a considerable discount from the retail figures used in this model. However, starting patients on TCAs remains more expensive up until an 85% discount, or $0.89 per week, is reached. This is largely because of the number of TCA patients who must be switched to more expensive second-line treatment (SSRIs).

One-year maintenance treatment

Maintenance or prophylactic treatment of depression is becoming increasingly important in psychiatry as the recurrent nature of the illness is better recognized (Maj *et al.*, 1992). Therefore an analysis of cost differences should consider maintenance treatment as well. To develop a realistic maintenance model we must first remember that the acute treatment model was developed assuming that patients had never received pharmacological treatment for depression. This assumption made it reasonable to start patients with either a TCA or SSRI. If they *had* undergone previous treatment, that history would significantly influence treatment selection.

The assumption of no previous treatment is also relevant to the maintenance model, since the main indication for maintenance treatment is a history of one or more clinically significant episodes of depression. Very few patients will present with a history of one or more significant major depressive episodes but have never taken an antidepressant. Therefore in this model very few patients will be extended into maintenance treatment.

The outline of the maintenance model can be simply described. A percentage of the patients on maintenance will drop out. A portion of these dropouts and a smaller percentage of the remaining patients will relapse. The relapsers will require more doctor visits, and some of the relapses will be hospitalized. The relapsers will also be switched to the other antidepressant if they have not previously failed a trial with it.

The estimates used in this model are derived, where possible, from the available literature (Rouillon *et al.*, 1992; Montgomery and Montgomery, 1992). It is estimated that 10% of acute patients will enter maintenance treatment and 10% of these patients will drop out during the year. There will be a 65% relapse rate for dropouts and a 25% relapse rate for compliant patients. The average time to dropout is estimated as six months. The average duration of treatment for patients who drop out and do not relapse is therefore six months. The duration of treatment for compliant patients is one year. For patients who relapse, it is six months plus an additional year. The estimates for rate of hospitalization, cost of hospitalization and extra doctor visits are the same as in the acute treatment model.

The model predicts that TCAs will be slightly less expensive than SSRIs ($1374) during maintenance treatment. If the cost advantage of SSRIs in acute treatment is added to the equation ($47 257) then SSRIs remain less expensive.

We tested the estimates used in the maintenance treatment model similar to the way we did for the acute treatment model. We looked for points at which the cost difference of the acute and maintenance phases favoured TCAs. We again found the model to be very robust. Starting patients on SSRIs remained more economical with hospitalization rates down to 5%, up to 29 office visits during initial treatment or $0 cost per visit.

Discussion

The model presented in this chapter compares the costs in drug-naive patients of SSRI treatment with generic TCAs. The null hypothesis was that treatment with the TCAs would be much less expensive than SSRI treatment. The projected costs allow us to reject the null hypothesis over a range of estimates. Even if patients are treated in a health care programme that does not include hospitalization benefits (i.e. a hospitalization rate of zero) the cost savings with TCAs is not large: $19 per patient over the acute period and $29 per patient during the acute and maintenance phases. Therefore there is no basis to conclude that starting treatment with SSRIs will be much more expensive than TCAs.

This conclusion is strengthened if one considers that a number of cost differences which favour SSRIs were not included in the model. The most dramatic is TCA overdose, which is the most common life-threatening drug ingestion in the USA. The in-hospital mortality ranges from 0.6% to 15% (Dec and Stern, 1990). Amitriptyline, imipramine, desipramine and nortriptyline are each associated with 30–150 deaths per million prescriptions in the UK (Henry, 1989). Together these data suggest that several patients per thousand prescribed a TCA may be hospitalized for a TCA overdose.

In contrast, SSRI overdose is relatively benign (Cooper, 1988; Kelvin and Hakansson, 1989; Borys *et al.*, 1990). To date only one successful suicide with fluoxetine alone has been reported despite millions of prescriptions (Kincaid *et al.*, 1990). Animal data and more limited human experience with overdoses of the other SSRIs suggest that good outcome after overdose is a quality of all the drugs in this class (Boyer and Blumhardt, 1992; Doogan and Caillard, 1988). SSRIs also do not augment the effects of alcohol or other sedatives when taken together in normal doses, and there are no data to suggest they do so in overdose (Schaffler, 1986; McClelland and Raptopoulos, 1985; Hindmarch and Harrison, 1988; Cooper *et al.*, 1989; Hindmarch *et al.*, 1990). Fluoxetine may, however, prolong the clearance of other psychotropics, such as TCAs, if taken in a combined ingestion. Sertraline is much less likely to do so (Cunningham *et al.*, 1992). The available data suggest that the risk of suicidal acts with SSRIs is no more, and possibly less, than with TCAs (Beasley *et al.*, 1991; Henry *et al.*, 1992). Therefore patients are no more likely to take an SSRI overdose, and if they do it is likely on the average to be much less serious and expensive than with TCAs.

Other serious TCA side effects are due to cardiotoxic, anticholinergic, anti-adrenergic and antihistamine effects, which SSRIs do not share. These side effects include cardiac arrhythmias, constipation with the risk of impaction, urinary obstruction, and delirium. Sedation may pose a risk when driving or operating heavy machinery (Hindmarch and Harrison, 1988). The use of TCAs in the elderly nearly doubles the risk of hip fractures, presumably due to orthostatic hypotension (Ray et al., 1987).

TCAs also predispose to dental caries and weight gain, both of which have cost implications (Rose and Westhead, 1967). Berken and colleagues (1984) found that patients gained an average of 1.3–2.9 pounds a month on TCAs in long-term treatment. Increased weight was also the most common reason given by their patients for discontinuing maintenance TCA therapy. SSRIs are not associated with weight gain. They are also not associated with dry mouth and therefore do not predispose to caries.

The SSRIs are still new enough that legal liabilities stemming from choice of treatment is not an issue. In the future physicians could find that the legal system holds them accountable for problems stemming from TCA treatment when safer alternatives are available. Such problems might include fatal overdose, motor vehicle accidents due to sedation, and falls.

The use of TCAs may also require greater expenditures for medical tests. These would include measurement of TCA plasma concentration and baseline ECGs for some patients. In contrast, SSRI plasma levels are rarely clinically useful. Baseline ECGs are seldom if ever necessary because of the SSRIs' lack of effect on cardiac conduction.

Several of the estimates used in the model come from clinical drug trials. These data may underestimate two factors which decrease the efficacy of an antidepressant: compliance and underdosing. Great emphasis is placed on compliance in studies by medication logs, pill counts and emphasis by the investigator. Underdosing is uncommon in trials since the dosage requirements are set at therapeutic levels and physicians are encouraged to increase the dose to these goals. Underdosing is likely to be more of a problem in clinical practice. Studies suggest that 75% of patients may be significantly underdosed and that compliance with TCAs may be as low as 20–32% in clinical practice (Johnson, 1981; Katon et al., 1992).

Two factors contribute to poor compliance with TCA treatment: side effects and the practice of prescribing TCAs in divided doses. Side effects, which are usually worse at the beginning of treatment, and delay in the onset of the therapeutic effect may discourage patients from staying on their medicine. Giving TCAs in divided doses is often an attempt to prevent or manage side effects.

Underdosing may result from lack of knowledge by the prescribing physician or represent an attempt to prevent or manage side effects. Underdosing also may result from the practice of gradually titrating TCA dosage. Patients may not increase their dose to a therapeutic level for a variety of reasons, including side effects, difficulty complying with a divided regimen, or ambivalence about treatment.

The factors which lead to underdosing of or non-compliance with TCAs are much less important for SSRIs, since serious side effects are much less common, divided dosing is rare, and dosage rarely requires titration.

There is another consideration. Almost all clinical antidepressant trials exclude patients with significant personality disorders or primary diagnoses other than major depression. However, in the real clinical world not all depressed patients fit this category. The available evidence suggests that SSRIs are more likely to be effective in a range of illnesses related to depression and in patients with personality disorders (Boyer, 1992). If so, this would boost the response rate to SSRIs, especially over a large number of patients.

This discussion has also not included occupational and societal costs. Wells and colleagues found that the impact of depression on physical, social and role functioning was the same or greater than that of the other serious chronic illnesses they examined. These included hypertension, diabetes, coronary artery disease, arthritis, back, lung or gastrointestinal disorders.

The total direct and indirect costs of depressive illness are large and are increasing. They were estimated to be $16.3 billion a year in 1986 (Stoudemire *et al.*, 1986) and $29 billion in 1991 (Abraham *et al.*, 1991). Depressive illness may also increase medical expenditures not usually considered to be directly related to depression. For example, outpatients with high levels of emotional distress are also likely to be high utilizers of health care (Katon *et al.*, 1990). Medical inpatients with clinically significant depression and anxiety have more procedures performed, 35% greater hospital costs, and 40% longer hospital stays (Levenson *et al.*, 1990). Elderly medical inpatients who are depressed also have greater in-hospital mortality and are more likely to be rehospitalized than those who are not (Koenig *et al.*, 1989). These observations suggest that more effective treatment of depression may reduce medical costs in these areas.

When treatment for depression is ineffective or not tolerated there is prolonged disability, which may lead to unemployment, loss of health benefits and lack of access to private health care. A downward spiral of general health status and increased reliance on government funds may then ensue. Von-Korff and colleagues (1992) showed that successful treatment of depression results in significant decreases in this disability. Ineffective treatment may also lead to job loss, family disruption, divorce and suicide.

Conclusions

This chapter has shown that starting treatment with generic TCAs in previously untreated patients is likely to be more expensive than starting with SSRIs. The main reason is patient acceptability. There are likely to be more treatment dropouts with TCAs. The dropouts will require a greater average number of office visits, some of them will require hospitalization, and most of them will need to start a full course of treatment with a more expensive alternative. TCAs also carry a higher risk of significant, and costly, major side effects. These cost projections plus risks of disability, job loss, family disruption, divorce and suicide mean there are strong financial and ethical arguments for initiating treatment with the medications most likely to be safe, tolerated and effective, such as the SSRIs.

References

Abraham IL, Neese JB and Westerman PS (1991) Depression: nursing implications of a clinical and social problem. *Nurs Clin North Am* **1991**, 527–544.

Beasley CM, Dornseif BE, Bosomowrth JC *et al.* (1991) Fluoxetine and suicide: a meta-analysis of controlled trials of treatment for depression. *Br Med J* **303**, 685–692.

Bentkover JD, Baker AM, Feighner JP and Wells BG (1992) Presented at the 18th CINP conference Nice, France, 28 June–2 July (submitted).

Berken GH, Weinstein DO and Stern WC (1984) Weight gain: a side effect of tricyclic antidepressants. *J Affect Disord* **7**, 133–138.

Blackwell B, Peterson GR, Kuzma RJ *et al.* (1980) The effect of five tricyclic antidepressants on salivary flow and mood in healthy volunteers. *Commun Psychopharmacol* **4**, 255–261.

Borys DJ, Setzer SC, Ling LJ *et al.* (1990) The effects of fluoxetine in the overdose patient. *J Toxicol Clin Toxicol* **28**, 331–340.

Boyer WF (1992) Potential indications for the SSRIs. *Int Clin Psychopharmacol* **6** (Suppl 5), 5–12.

Boyer WF and Blumhardt C (1992) The safety profile of paroxetine. *J Clin Psychiatry* **53**, 61–66.

Cooper, GL (1988) The safety of fluoxetine: an update. *Br J Psychiatry* **153**, 77–86.

Cooper SM, Jackson D, Loudon JM, McClelland GR and Raptopoulos P (1989) The psychomotor effects of paroxetine alone and in combination with haloperidol, amylobarbitone, oxazepam, or alcohol. *Acta Psychiatr Scand* **80**, 53–55.

Cunningham LA, Borison RL, Carman J, Crowder J and Diamond BI (1992) Comparison of venlafaxine, trazodone and placebo in major depression. *New Research Program and Abstracts,* American Psychiatric Association 145th Annual Meeting, p. 198.

Dec GW and Stern TA (1990) Tricyclic antidepressants in the intensive care unit. *J Intensive Care Med* **5**, 69–81.

Doogan DP and Caillard V (1988) Sertraline: a new antidepressant. *J Clin Psychiatry* **49**, 46–51.

Henry JA (1989) A fatal toxicity index for antidepressant poisoning. *Acta Psychiatr Scan Suppl* **80** (Suppl. 354), 37–45.

Henry EW, Chandler LP, Burnside R, Doogan DP and Salsburg D (1992) Evaluation of suicidality in the sertraline, placebo, and active control groups in the sertraline depression program. *Clin Neuropharmacol* **15**, 82.

Hindmarch I and Harrison C (1988) The effects of paroxetine and other antidepressants in combination with alcohol in psychomotor activity related to car driving. *Hum Psychopharmacol* **3**, 13–20.

Hindmarch I, Shillingford J and Shillingford C (1990) The effects of sertraline on psychomotor performance in elderly volunteers *J Clin Psychiatry* **51**, 34–36.

Jenike MA (1989) Treatment of affective illness in the elderly with drugs and electroconvulsive therapy. *J Geriatr Psychiatry* **22**, 77–112.

Johnson DAW (1981) Depression: treatment compliance in general practice. *Acta Psychiatr Scand* **63**, 447–453.

Katon W, von-Korff M, Lin E *et al.* (1990) Distressed high utilizers of medical care: DSM-III-R diagnoses and treatment needs. *Gen Hosp Psychiatry* **12**, 355–362.

Katon W, von Korff M, Lin E, Bush T and Ormel J (1992) Adequacy and duration of antidepressant treatment in primary care. *Med Care* **30**, 67–76.

Kelvin AS and Hakansson S (1989) Comparative acute toxicity of paroxetine and other antidepressants. *Acta Psychiatr Scan Suppl* **80**, 31–33.

Kincaid RL, McMullin MM, Crookham SB and Rieders F (1990) Report of a fluoxetine fatality. *J Anal Toxicol* **14**, 327–329.

Koenig HG, Shelp F, Goli V, Cohen HJ and Blazer DG (1989) Survival and health care utilization in elderly medical inpatients with major depression. *J Am Geriatr Soc* **37**, 599–606.

Levenson JL, Hamer RM and Rossiter LF (1990) Relation of psychopathology in general medical inpatients to use and cost of services. *Am J Psychiatry* **147**, 1498–1503.

Maj M, Veltro F, Pirozzi R, Lobrace S and Magliano L (1992) Pattern of recurrence of illness after recovery from an episode of major depression: a prospective study. *Am J Psychiatry* **149**, 795–800.

McClelland GR and Raptopoulos P (1985) Psychomotor effects of paroxetine and amitriptyline, alone and in combination with ethanol. *Br J Clin Pharmacol* **19**, 578.

McCombs JS, Nichol MB, Stimmel GL *et al.* (1990) The cost of antidepressant drug therapy failure: a study of antidepressant use patterns in a Medicaid population. *J Clin Psychiatry* **51**, 60–69.

McCue RE (1992) Using tricyclic antidepressants in the elderly. *Clin Geriatr Med* **8**, 323–334.

Montgomery SA and Montgomery DB (1992) Prophylactic treatment in recurrent unipolar depression. In: Montgomery SA and Rouillon F (eds) *Long-term Treatment of Depression*, pp. 53–80, Chichester: Wiley.

Ray WA, Griffin MR, Schaffner W, Baugh DK and Melton LJ (1987) Psychotropic drug use and the risk of hip fractures. *N Engl J Med* **316**, 363–369.

Roose SP, Glassman AH, Giardina EG *et al.* (1987) Tricyclic antidepressants in depressed patients with cardiac conduction disease. *Arch Gen Psychiatry* **44**, 273–275.

Rose JT and Westhead TT (1967) Treatment of depression: a comparative trial of imipramine and desipramine. *Br J Psychiatry* **113**, 659–665.

Rouillon F, Lefoyeux M and Filteau MJ (1992) Unwanted effects of long-term treatment. In: Montgomery S and Rouillon F (eds) *Long-term Treatment of Depression*, pp. 81–112. Chichester: Wiley.

Schaffler K (1986) Study on performance and alcohol interaction with the antidepressant fluoxetine—a selective serotonin reuptake inhibitor—using computer assisted psychophysiological methodology. *Br J Clin Pract* **40**, 28–33.

Seppala T, Linnoila M (1983) Effects of zimeldine and other antidepressants on skilled performance: a comprehensive review. *Acta Psychiatr Scand* **68**, 135–140.

Settle EC (1992) Antidepressant side effects: issues and options. *J Clin Psychiatry Monograph* **10**, 48–61.

Stoudemire A, Frank R, Hedemark N *et al.* (1986) The economic burden of depression. *Gen Hosp Psychiatry* **8**, 387–394.

Von-Korff M, Ormel J, Katon W and Lin EHB (1992) Disability and depression among high utilizers of health care: a longitudinal analysis. *Arch Gen Psychiatry* **49**, 91–100.

6

Outcomes, costs and design of health insurance for depression

Thomas G. McGuire

Introduction

This chapter integrates services research with clinical research on depression to characterize trade-offs in payment system design. It is self-evident that more generous insurance increases costs and that all potentially useful services cannot be made available at no charge to users. Choices must be made between providing the greatest access to services and presumably the most favourable outcomes on the one hand, and limiting costs of treatment on the other. Payment systems are multifaceted creatures, with demand and supply-side components and many variations of cost-sharing strategies. Responses to payment system changes are themselves complex, and in many areas not well understood. Documenting the cost and effectiveness trade-offs through payment system design must be recognized as a difficult task. The state of research is such that cost impacts can be forecast more reliably than impacts on the effectiveness of treatment.

Depression is one of the most common forms of mental illness. Six per cent of the population are clinically depressed in a six-month period. Furthermore, major depression is the most prevalent major mental illness. In both minor and major forms, depression is disabling. Depression is, however, intermittent; most

* This chapter is based on research conducted in connection with contract H3-6690.1 from the Office of Technology Assessment (OTA). Analysis and conclusions in this chapter are the responsibility of the author alone.

Health Economics of Depression. Edited by B. Jönsson and J. Rosenbaum
© 1993 John Wiley & Sons Ltd.

people suffering from depression are healthy most of the time, able to work and play normal roles in family and social life. Indeed, for about half the people with a major depressive episode, the first episode will be their last. Paying for treatment for depression is mainly a private responsibility. Depression is the most costly mental illness for private insurance, although limits on insurance coverage force many families to pay a substantial share of costs.

Clinical Background

Defining depression

The *Diagnostic and Statistical Manual, Third Edition* (DSM-III-R) of the American Psychiatric Association contains no disease labelled simply 'depression' but several depression-related conditions more specifically defined within the broader classification of affective disorders (see American Psychiatric Association, 1987). An affective disorder is a 'disturbance of mood, accompanied by a full or partial manic or depressive syndrome that is not due to any other physical or mental disorders' (American Psychiatric Association, 1980, p. 205). Within the subgroups of Major Affective Disorders, Other Specific Affective Disorders, and Atypical Affective Disorders, a depressive form is paired with a form featuring both depressed and manic affect.

In common usage, 'depression' covers a range of personal moods from a mild case of the blues to more serious conditions that interfere with personal and social functioning. Psychiatric classifications rely on the number of specific symptoms of depression, the persistence in those symptoms over time, and their cause to differentiate the forms of depression. Psychiatrists agree that major depression is a very heterogeneous condition or group of conditions.

Although all persons meeting criteria for some form of depression have depressive symptoms, it should be clear that nor all persons with depressive symptoms merit a psychiatric diagnosis of some form of depression. Nonetheless, as Wells (1985) points out, those with symptoms as well as those with a proper DSM-III-R disorder may be of policy significance. Persons with some depressive symptoms not suffering from some form of depression as currently defined may, for example, suffer from disability due to the symptoms, overuse general medical services, or benefit from treatment.

Recent studies have emphasized that depressive symptoms even in the absence of a DSM-III-R diagnosis have clinical implications. Broadhead *et al.* (1990) used data from the Epidemiologic Catchment Area (ECA) Study in North Carolina and operationalized categories of 'minor depression'—individuals with some depressive symptoms but not qualifying for one of the DSM-III-R conditions. They distinguished between those with and without a mood disturbance. Persons with a minor depression with a mood disturbance had an elevated probability of moving to a major depressive episode and experienced three times the number of disability days during a later period than asymptomatic individuals.

In the Medical Outcome Study (MOS) being conducted by researchers at the Rand Corporation, major depression and dysthymia are employed as one of several tracer conditions to evaluate the performance of alternative organizational and financing arrangements for providing medical care. Patients with depressive symptoms (with and without disorders) were compared with patients reporting one of eight chronic conditions. With the exception of current heart disease, depression was at least as disabling and had at least as great an impact on patient well-being as diabetes, hypertension, arthritis, gastrointestinal problems, lung problems or back problems (Wells *et al.*, 1989b).

It is worth keeping in mind that even if depression is best thought about as being continuous on some dimensions, it is not necessarily continuous on all. Patients with a major depressive episode may merit aggressive medication-based treatment, for example; it may not be true that those with lesser symptoms should receive medication in smaller doses.

The prevalence and treated prevalence of depression

In 1977, at the initiation of work of the President's Commission for Mental Health, Rosalynn Carter would ask 'How many are mentally ill? Who are they? How are they treated? Psychiatric epidemiologists had no satisfactory answers. Although the prevalence of psychiatric disorders has been studied for many years, criteria for disease applied during the 1950s no longer reflected current thinking. In the Stirling County Study (Leighton *et al.*, 1963) and the Midtown Manhattan Study (Srole *et al.*, 1962), lifetime prevalence was estimated at 57% and 81%. Numbers from these earlier studies were simply not believable.

The National Institute of Mental Health (NIMH) sponsored development of a reliable instrument to be used to detect psychiatric disorder in the community based on DSM-III disease criteria—the Diagnostic Interview Schedule (DIS)—and sponsored a five-site project to document disease—the Epidemiologic Catchment Area (ECA) Study. In an overview paper in Robins and Regier (1991), Robins *et al.* (1991) call estimates from the ECA 'the best current estimates of the prevalence of psychiatric disorders in American', a claim that has not met dispute. Based on all five sites, estimates are that 32% of persons have experienced a psychiatric disorder at some point during their lifetime, and the annual prevalence of disease is 20%.

Information from the ECA is reported in different formats in different publications. Most useful for our discussion is when diseases are grouped as in Taube and Barett (1985), containing data from three sites: New Haven, CT, Baltimore, MD, and St Louis, MO.

As shown in Table I, the six-month prevalence of any DIS/DSM-III disorder is estimated at 18.7%. Anxiety/somatoform disorders and substance abuse disorders are slightly more prevalent than affective disorders. During a six-month

Table I.   Six-month prevalence of DIS/DSM-III disorders among adults (18+). Three ECA sites: first wave.

Disorder	Prevalance (%)
Any DIS disorder	18.7
Any DIS disorder except phobia	14.4
Any DIS disorder except substance abuse	14.0
Substance abuse disorders	6.4
Alcohol abuse/dependence	5.0
Drug abuse/dependence	2.0
Schizophrenic/schizophreniform	1.0
Affective disorders	6.0
Manic episodes	0.7
Major depressive episode	3.1
Dysthemia	3.2
Anxiety/somatoform disorders	8.3
Phobia	7.0
Panic	0.8
Obsessive compulsive	1.5
Somatization	0.1
Antisocial personality	0.9
Cognitive impairment (severe)	1.0

Source: Taube and Barrett (1985).

period, it is estimated that 6% of the population will have a DIS/DSM-III diagnosis of an affective disorder. The most prevalent types of affective disorder are major depressive episode and dysthymia, each affecting about 3% of the population during a six-month period.

The ECA study also collected data on service use of survey participants. A striking finding of the survey is the relatively low rate of use of mental health services among persons with a DIS/DSM-III disorder. Overall, as Table II shows, only 17.6% of the persons with a DIS/DSM-III disorder had a mental health visit during the six months prior to the survey. Only 9.9% saw a mental health specialist. Mechanic (1990) raises some important cautions in connection with these data. As he points out, absence of a visit during the preceding six months could be due to many factors, including 'unawareness of the need for treatment, a rejection of treatment, or a particular stage in the illness and care trajectory' Mechanic (1990, p. 64). Mechanic also points out that the ECA data may overstate the role of the general medical sector. The format for the question for persons visiting the general medical sector was essentially, 'During the visit did you talk to the doctor about problems with your emotions or nerves?' A 'yes' to this does not imply that the mental problem was the main reason for the visit, nor does it imply that any more than superficial attention was devoted to the problem by the practitioner.

Table II.   Percentage of ambulatory health and/or mental health visits in past six months for person with specific recent DIS/DSM-III disorders: three-site average.

Disorder	Percentage with visit (%)
Any DIS disorders covered	
All types of visits	67.3
Mental health visits (total)	17.6
General medical provider only	7.7
Mental health specialist	9.9
Substance abuse/dependence	
All types of visits	58.8
Mental health visits (total)	13.6
General medical provider only	3.6
Mental health specialist	10.0
Schizophrenic/schizophreniform disorders	
All types of visits	77.7
Mental health visits (total)	46.7
General medical provider only	9.0
Mental health specialist	37.7
Affective disorders	
All types of visits	77.6
Mental health visits (total)	31.4
General medical provider only	13.8
Mental health specialist	17.6
Anxiety/somatoform disorders	
All types of visits	73.9
Mental health visits (total)	20.3
General medical provider only	8.9
Mental health specialist	11.4
Antisocial personality	
All types of visits	77.2
Mental health visits (total)	23.0
General medical provider only	8.2
Mental health specialist	14.8
Cognitive impairment (severe)	
All types of visits	51.2
Mental health visits (total)	6.1
General medical provider only	2.8
Mental health specialist	3.2

Source: Taube and Barrett (1985).

It is interesting to compare the rates of mental health visits of those persons with and without a recent DIS/DSM-III disorder, as is done in Table III. Those with a disorder make much more frequent use of mental health care. Those with a recent DIS/DSM-III disorder are roughly four times more likely to make a

Table III.   Percentage of ambulatory health and/or mental health visits in past six months for persons with and without any recent DIS/DSM-III disorders: three-site average.

	With recent disorder (%)	Without recent disorder (%)	All persons (%)
Any mental health visit	17.6	4.1	6.6
General medical only	7.7	2.4	3.4
Mental health specialist	9.9	1.7	3.2

Implications

● Of the 6.6% of the population who make a mental health visit in a six-month period, 50.0% have no DIS/DSM–III disorder

● Of the 3.4% of the population who make a mental health visit to a general medical provider only, 57.6% have no DIS/DSM–III disorder

● Of the 3.2% of the population who make a visit to a mental health specialist, 42.1% have no DIS/SDM–III disorder

Source: Shapiro *et al.* (1984).

mental health visit. However, there are of course many more people without a recent DIS/DSM-III disorder than there are with a disorder. Although the rates of use in the disorder-free group are much lower, the larger base implies that a large share of the persons in treatment have no recent disorder. As noted at the bottom of Table III, half of persons receiving a mental health visit have no recent disorder, including over 40% of those in treatment by a mental health specialist.

Health insurance, cost, risk, access and outcomes

The costs of treatment for depression can be very large. Two episodes of hospitalization, which may occur in the same year, can require 50–70 days of treatment, and cost perhaps $30 000–$40 000. Over a longer period, the costs of treatment for serious depression will continue to mount. These costs are a risk against which individuals and families will want protection. Private insurance covers some costs. Public programmes such as Medicare and Medicaid pay some costs on behalf of the elderly, disabled and poor. Persons without private or public payment sources must rely on the public mental health systems to provide treatment when necessary. In general, individuals and families are more exposed to the financial risk associated with depression than for other major physical illnesses.

Historically, mental health care has been subject to special coverage restrictions in health insurance for a number of reasons. (1) Mental health care is perceived to be ineffective. (2) The demand response to insurance for mental health care exceeds the demand response for other medical conditions. (3) Public mental hospitals and clinics provide treatment for uninsured mental patients. (4) Good mental health coverage may attract bad risks to the benefit plan. These reasons cannot be discussed in detail here. It is worth noting, however, that evidence for the effectiveness of some treatment for depression is solid. The cost factors inhibiting coverage are the subject of this section.

There are many parameters of a health payment plan, involving demand-side cost sharing (e.g., coinsurance and deductibles), supply-side cost sharing (e.g., prospective payment), and managed care. Although some of these instruments can have powerful effects on use and cost, it must be kept in mind that these are limited tools. Changing the health payment system (at least in the short run, and certainly if the changes apply to only a relatively small part of the health care system) will not alter the basic attitudes of patients and families, and the under-lying outlook and technology of the professionals making decisions about treat-ment. More generous insurance will not cure the problem that well less than half of patients with depression in a six-month period sought treatment of any kind. There are no magic bullets in the payment system holster to remedy the inappropriate treatment professionals bring to bear on depression—too little treatment in some cases, and too much treatment, especially unnecessary res-idential treatment, in others.

Payment systems affect behaviour around the edges of patterns of demand and supply of services determined by other forces. Eisenberg (1992) cites the tend-ency of patients in primary care practice to somatize their problems, defining their problem in terms of physical discomfort rather than emotional distress. Primary care physicians often collude with patients in ignoring psychological issues, the physicians preferring to ignore the psychological component of a patient's prob-lem because of their own lack of training or attitudes, or because of inadequate incentives to take the time to diagnosis and manage the mental illness.

In this section, we describe baseline behaviour of an insured group in terms of the patterns of cost and treatment for depression that reflects prevailing tendencies of patients and physicians to ignore depression and other mental illnesses. The effects of feasible payment system changes on use and cost are forecast. These effects are then interpreted in light of the epidemiology of depression and in light of what is known about effective treatment. We examine demand-side cost-sharing for inpatient and office-based care, and supply-side cost-sharing for inpatient care. Unfortunately, research is unavailable to support forecasts of changes in behaviour as the result of changes in the physician fees.

Insurance benefits for depression treatment at company X
Baseline utilization of treatment for depression is taken from the 1989 claims experience of 'company X', a manufacturing and services company in a mid-western state. Study of company X confers several advantages. Coverage for mental illness at the company is very generous, approximately at parity with other conditions. Mental hospitalization is essentially completely covered. Par-tial hospitalization is a covered benefit. Outpatient psychotherapy is also

covered without limit. There is a fee limit on plan payments, however, that imply an effective coinsurance of about 27%. Generous coverage means that all utilization can be 'seen' in a claims data set. Second, company X employs managed care and a preferred provider organization (PPO), although data do not permit estimation of the effects of these plan features. Third, data have been provided in a per person summary form, so that some elements of the relation between inpatient and outpatient use can be studied, and risk at the person level can be assessed.

A major limitation of the data is that it is impossible to check the validity of the diagnostic information or to verify the necessity of the services provided—a limitation which is shared by any claims data set. This limit on the validity of clinical information available to a payer is a fundamental problem for insurance policy (not just research). Insurers must deal with the world as reported on claims forms; in that sense, these data are highly relevant.

According to the ICD-9 diagnostic information recorded on hospital claims, one-third of mental health and substance abuse discharges were for Affective Psychoses. (Diagnostic data on outpatient claims were unavailable, and would in any case be of highly questionable validity.) Assuming that one-third of the patients treated for a mental health or substance abuse disorder suffer from depression implies that 909 patients received mental health treatment for depression during a year. Annual prevalence of DSM-III depression can be conservatively estimated at 6% (see Table I) of the covered population of 53 200 or 3192. A treatment rate of 909/3192 = 28% is in the range discovered in the ECA data (Table II). If we recognize that many of those treated will not have DSM-III diagnosis, the rate of treatment might fall to near the 17% found for affective disorders in the ECA study. It is not known how many patients may have been under treatment by general physicians who never billed for a mental health procedure.

Table IV summarizes the treatment the 909 patients received during 1989. Most patients, 750/909 or 82%, were treated as outpatients only. About 75% (682/909) of all patients treated incurred covered charges of less than $2000 for outpatient treatment only. Seventeen per cent (111+48)/909 were discharged from a hospital at some point during the year. A small portion of the treated population used more than 30 hospital days during a year. The 159 persons treated for some hospitalization accounted for 190 discharges during the year. The average length of stay was 28 days. Among the patients discharged during the year, a significant number have no outpatient mental health procedures. Although intermediate levels of care (such as partial hospitalization) are a covered benefit, these were used by very few persons treated for mental illness in company X. (Partial hospitalization could not be separately identified in the claims and is included in the inpatient figures. Information on the infrequency of use of partial hospitalization came from the insurer for company X.) It is clear from Table IV that payment system changes will have different effects on patients depending on what treatment they are receiving. Changes in hospital payment policy will have virtually no effect, for example, on the 80% of the treated individuals not using hospital care. In the analysis that follows, we will study the effect of payment system changes on three groups of patients defined as follows:

Group I: heavy inpatient users, those with 31+ days of hospital care in a year.
Group II: moderate inpatient users, those with 1–30 hospital days in a year.
Group III: outpatient users, those treated for depression as outpatients but with
    no inpatient care.

Members of all three groups will use outpatient care. By definition, all members of group III use outpatient care and none use hospitalization. As the bottom of Table IV makes clear, the main difference in utilization is with respect to inpatient care. Average inpatient use for group I is 61 days, compared to 14.5 for group II and none for group III. Patients in one group in 1989 may be in another in 1990 or, indeed, be untreated. It is also recognized that payment system features can affect the likelihood of individuals appearing in the various groups.

Table V summarizes cost information group by group. As expected, group I has by far the highest inpatient costs. Group I is 5% of the treated population but accounts for 50% of the total costs of treatment for depression. See also Figure 1 for display of these important data. In total, depression treatment for these 909 patients cost $2.9 million in 1989.

Table VI shows the division of costs between plan-paid and uninsured in the present plan for company X and selected alternative payment plans. The present plan in section VI(a) leaves few costs uninsured. Company X patients are essentially fully insured for hospital care (small coinsurance for some initial use before a stop-loss is ignored in this analysis). Outpatient care has a copayment feature induced by the company fee limit, but on average for each group the

Table IV.   Joint distribution of inpatient and outpatient use, company X, 1989.

		Inpatient		
	None	1–30 days	31+ days	Total
Outpatient				
None		40	10	50
$1000–2000	682	65	28	775
$2001+	68	6	10	84
Total	750	111	48	909
% no. outpt	NA	36%	20%	
Avg. days		14.5	61.0	
Avg. outpt	$831	$530	$990	

Table V.   Summary of costs by groups, company X, 1989.

	Group I Hvy input	Group II Mod. input	Group III Outpt	All
Number	48	111	750	909
% of total	5.2%	12.2%	82.5%	
Per person costs				
Inpatient	$29 097	$6937	$0	$2374
Outpatients	$990	$530	$831	$803
Total	$30 087	$7467	$831	$3176
Total costs				
Costs (000s)	$1434	$829	$623	$2886
Percentage	49.7%	28.7%	21.6%	

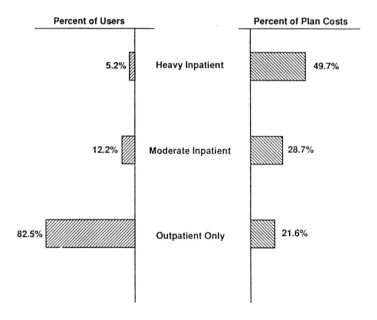

Figure 1.   Distribution of users and costs, company X, 1989.

uninsured costs are all less than $300. On average, company X spends $2954 per person treated for depression. Plan costs are of course much higher for group I members.

Use and cost in alternative payment plans
These data can be used to study plan alternatives that might be more realistic from a public policy perspective than the generous coverage presently in place

at company X. The purpose is not to analyse what company X should do, but to study the consequences for use and cost of payment plan alternatives that would put some limits on cost and use. The first alternative studied is a common cost-limiting tactic in private health insurance, limiting coverage to 30 days in a calendar year. Section (b) of Table VI summarizes the estimated cost impact.

The effects of a 30-day limit are very concentrated. In terms of users, the effect is obviously concentrated exclusively on group I—those using more than 30 days in a year. The average uninsured costs for this group of presumably most seriously ill individuals goes up to $5000 per year. All of these costs are of course associated with extended hospital treatment that is due to a combination of long stays and rehospitalizations. Some patients in group I will have uninsured costs of much more than $5000. Uninsured costs may be paid by the family or shifted to the public sector. Uninsured costs for extended hospitalization are particularly vulnerable to shifting to public budgets.

A 30-day limit conveys no incentives to economize on hospital care less than 30 days. About 40% of all hospitalization is consumed by members of group II who are not affected at all by the 30-day limit. The limit does result in plan savings of about 17% of total costs. It is possible that some members of group I would increase charges for outpatient care after imposition of a 30-day limit, making the 17 an upper estimate.

Section (c) of Table VI imposes a form of supply-side cost-sharing for inpatient care and some demand-side cost-sharing in the form of a one-day deductible to compare with the simple 30-day limit form of demand-side cost-sharing in section (b) of the table. Supply-side cost sharing is as in the TEFRA payment system for psychiatric facilities in Medicare. (TEFRA is the Tax Equity and Fiscal Responsibility Act of 1982. About 300 000 discharges are paid by Medicare each year using the TEFRA system.) TEFRA is roughly a 50 : 50 mix of cost-based and prospective reimbursement. The estimated supply response to TEFRA in comparison to cost-based reimbursement in the present plan is a 17% reduction in length of stay per episode (Harrow and Ellis, 1992). Medicare requires a one-day deductible (and 20% coinsurance) for hospital care, although most beneficiaries have supplemental insurance to cover these costs. The 'Model Plan' for mental health benefits developed for NIMH employs a mixed payment system for inpatient and other facility-based care similar in principle to TEFRA, and requires a one-day deductible per inpatient stay (Goldman *et al.*, 1992).

Saving under the TEFRA/one-day deductible option match the savings from a 30-day limit. The savings are achieved in very different ways, however, with different implications of use and access and uninsured costs. The uninsured costs created for group I are much lower under the TEFRA/deductible option. The average uninsured costs for a member of group I is only $1362 per year— much less than the $5000 falling on members of this group with a 30-day limit. Furthermore, the upper limit on uninsured costs is also much lower since it is determined by the number of hospitalizations, not the number of days above 30

Table VI.   Per person costs in present plan and alternatives, company X, 1989.

		Group I Hvy input	Group II Mod. input	Group III Outpt	All
(a)	*Present plan*				
	Inpt plan	$29 097	$6937	$0	
	Inpt unins.	$0	$0	$0	
	Inpt total	$29 097	$6937	$0	
	Outpt plan	$715	$383	$600	
	Outpt unins.	$275	$147	$231	
	Outpt total	$990	$530	$831	
	Total plan	$29 812	$7320	$600	$2954
	Total unins.	$275	$147	$231	$223
	Total	$30 087	$7467	$831	$3176
(b)	*30-day annual limit*				
	Inpt Plan	$19 594	$6937	$0	
	Inpt unins.	$4751	$0	$0	
	Inpt total	$24 346	$6937	$0	
	Outpt plan	$715	$383	$600	
	Outpt unins.	$275	$147	$231	
	Outpt total	$990	$530	$831	
	Total plan	$20 309	$7320	$600	$2455
	Total unins.	$5026	$147	$231	$472
	Total	$25 335	$7437	$831	$2927
		Plan saving		16.9%	
(c)	*TEFRA payment and one-day deductible*				
	Inpt plan	$23 063	$5499	$0	
	Input unins.	$1087	$259	$0	
	Inpt total	$24 151	$5758	$0	
	Outpt plan	$715	$383	$600	
	Outpt unins.	$275	$147	$231	
	Outpt total	$990	$530	$831	
	Total plan	$23 778	$5881	$600	$2461
	Total unins.	$1362	$406	$231	$312
	Total	$25 140	$6288	$831	$2773
		Plan saving		16.7%	
(d)	*Outpatient limit of $2000*				
	Inpt plan	$29 097	$6937	$0	
	Input unins.	$0	$0	$0	
	Inpt total	$29 097	$6937	$0	
	Outpt plan	$497	$316	$495	
	Outpt unins.	$346	$167	$262	
	Outpt total	$990	$530	$831	
	Total plan	$29 576	$7254	$495	$2847
	Total unins.	$346	$167	$262	$255
	Total	$30 087	$7467	$831	$3176
		Plan saving		3.6%	

Table VI. (*cont.*)

		Group I Hvy input	Group II Mod. input	Group III Outpt	All
(e)	*50% Cost sharing for outpatient*				
	Inpt plan	$29 097	$6937	$0	
	Inpt unins.	$0	$0	$0	
	Inpt total	$29 097	$6937	$0	
	Outpt plan	$412	$220	$346	
	Outpt unins.	$412	$220	$346	
	Outpt total	$823	$441	$692	
	Total plan	$29 509	$7158	$346	$2708
	Total unins.	$412	$220	$346	$334
	Total	$29 920	$7378	$692	$3042
	Plan saving		8.3%		

in a year. Even with four hospitalizations and the average amount of outpatient uninsured costs, the family or patient pays only $2183 out-of-pocket. Cost-shifting on to the public sector is much less likely when the cost sharing applies to the first day of hospitalization rather than the last days.

Incentives to economize on hospital care are spread uniformly across all hospital utilization under this supply-side cost-sharing alternative. For every hospital day, from the first to the last, the facility bears a share of the marginal cost. This facility share is 50% in a 50 : 50 mixed system, and roughly 50% on average under TEFRA. Incentives to economize apply to long and short hospitalizations, and thus to members of groups I and II. It is not assumed in Table VI that the deductible discourages any inpatient care or shifts any care to the outpatient sector. If it did, the estimated savings are an understatement of the full savings.

The 30-day limit and the TEFRA/one-day deductible for inpatient care are equivalent in terms of plan costs. How do they compare on other dimensions: risk to patients and families and encouraging use of cost-effective care? The TEFRA/one-day deductible is clearly superior from a risk standpoint. Families are limited in their financial exposure, and do not face any risk of financial ruin due to mental health treatment costs. A 30-day limit places a high burden on average on members of group I and exposes them to essentially unlimited up-side risk. Multiple years of membership in group I will ruin most working families. A corollary of this finding is the reduced risk of cost shifting to the public sector. Patients in ruined families still require care, and will turn to the public sector to get it.

Access to cost-effective treatment is harder to judge, but a case can be made that the incentives in the TEFRA/one-day deductible will lead to more appropriate use of inpatient care. Most observers believe, and this is supported by the evidence discussed above, that the heavy use of hospitalization in company X, while typical, is not necessary. Much of the care of patients with serious depression can be handled without residential treatment, or with briefer hospitalizations. Both alternatives studied reduce hospitalization in comparison to the full-insurance/cost-based payment scenario in the present plan. The 30-day annual limit alternative targets the change on days after 30 per year, having no direct effect on incentives up to that point. There is no disincentive for the first hospitalization during a year, and very strong disincentives for a second if the first approached 30 days of treatment. In comparison, the TEFRA/one-day deductible gives a moderate disincentive to hospital treatment (in comparison to full insurance) since the patient pays for the first day of treatment. After the decision to admit is made, incentives to economize on intensity of treatment and length of stay fall on the facility. The on/off nature of the incentives in the 30-day limit alternative is probably more distorting to access to effective treatment than the TEFRA/deductible incentives which apply continuously throughout utilization decisions. The TEFRA/deductible approach is applicable to intermediate forms of care, and is applied to partial hospitalization and related options in Frank *et al.* (1992).

'Managed care' is an option not analysed numerically here, but is another option for reducing reliance on inpatient care. Company X already employs a prior approval system for non-emergency admissions and continued care, so more strict management of care would be necessary to generate any savings. There is not a body of research that would allow us to make such estimates at this time (Hodgkin, 1992).

Sections (d) and (e) of Table VI analyse the effects of changes in demand-side cost-sharing for outpatient care. Section (d) estimates the effects of putting a $2000 limit on covered charges, roughly corresponding to a 20-visit limit per year. The effects of this change are fairly small in terms of overall plan costs, reducing them by an estimated 4%. Demand response assumptions are that demand falls linearly with cost-sharing and that use with no insurance is 30% of use with full insurance. Detailed information on the distribution of demand is contained in McGuire (1991). Uncovered costs rise slightly for all groups. From Table IV above it is evident that this limit would directly affect about 10% of the persons treated for depression. Section (e) increases the cost-sharing to 50% for outpatient care. The effective cost sharing was already 27% in the plan, so this constitutes a rough doubling of the rate. A 50% rate is the demand-side cost-sharing contained in Frank *et al.* (1992), and is that recommended by Manning *et al.* (1989) based on analysis of the Rand Health Insurance Experiment experience. An across-the-board 50% cost-sharing rate generates more plan savings— about 8%. Incentives to economize on outpatient treatment are increased for all visits, not just those after 20 as in the $2000 limit option.

While there is some evidence for the effectiveness of psychotherapy for treatment of depression, the high demand respond to insurance has hampered extension of coverage for psychotherapy to levels on a par with other office-based procedures in health benefit plans. Even the most seriously ill depressed patients do not make much more use of outpatient psychotherapy than do non-hospitalized patients. The average outpatient charges are $990 for group I compared with $831 for group III in Table V. High cost-sharing on outpatient treatment can be employed without exposing families or patients to extensive financial risk. The average uninsured costs in group I for outpatient costs is about $400 with a 50% cost-sharing.

Conclusion

This chapter studies the relation of insurance coverage (and other payment system features) to costs, access and outcomes for persons with depression. A payment system for health care affects health outcomes and the costs of the care in an indirect way by affecting service utilization. It has been necessary to centre the study on service utilization as the variable mediating between the policy—payment system choice—and the consequences of interest—outcomes and costs. We have been concerned with the effectiveness of services, with the costs of services, and with the effects of payment systems on the pattern of services use.

The literature on effectiveness and on the impact of payment systems on service use is largely distinct. With the exception of a couple of studies coming from the Rand Health Insurance Experiment (with null results), no research directly relates payment systems to outcomes. There are large numbers of studies, however, that make one of the two connections of interest. Effectiveness research ties services to outcomes, and research in economics and mental health ties payment systems to services.

A payment system for depression or mental health treatment more broadly must deal with multiple objectives and be set in recognition of behaviour in the real world, not the research setting. Goals of a health payment system include:

- Giving patients access to services providing the best outcomes.
- minimizing cost of services.
- protecting patients and families from financial risk.

All three goals cannot be met simultaneously. The major purpose of this chapter is to use research evidence from epidemiology, clinical studies and services research to characterize the trade-offs among the goals as clearly as possible. The sharpness of the trade-offs among these objectives is determined by the use of treatment for depression in the real world. We have given a sense of this by examination of the treatment for depression in the case of company X.

The main lessons were:

1. In a payment system with demand-side cost-sharing roughly at parity with other medical services, and no supply-side cost-sharing, treatment for depression is expensive, and expense is concentrated on hospital care for a small group of patients treated.
2. A 'basic benefit' with very limited annual inpatient days and high demand-side cost-sharing on psychotherapy can reduce costs substantially but at the same time impose financial risk on families or shift costs to the public sector.
3. Comparable plan costs to the limited basic benefit are achievable by a Medicare-type benefit with Medicare-type supply-side cost-sharing. Cost-shifting to the public sector is avoided. Financial risk to families is low.

In sum, based on the analyses of a company with patterns of treatment of depression that are typical of patterns in private health insurance, payment systems that meet high standards on all three objectives—providing access to necessary care, containing costs, and protecting families against financial risk—are clearly feasible.

None of the alternatives considered in the previous section confront the major problem that many persons with depression go untreated. Labelling this an 'access' problem reflects a preconception that increasing the supply of practitioners or reducing the price will address the problem. There is frankly no evidence that this is so. Taking the data from company X, for example, in spite of the virtually unimpeded 'access' available to persons covered in this plan, significant numbers of persons with depression go untreated, and, among those treated, there appears to be under-use of alternatives to hospital care.

An important conclusion from this is that, at least based on these data, insurance coverage for outpatient care and for alternatives alone will not cure the 'access' problem. Inadequate reimbursements are another possibility, as are underlying attitudes of patients and attitudes and training of providers. It is not known how payment changes to physicians will alter their rate of detection and treatment. Common sense suggests that an adequate rate of payment for the time and effort to diagnose and manage depression (and other mental illnesses) is a necessary condition for adequate supply, but is unlikely to be sufficient.

Existing evidence on effectiveness and behaviour of providers and users of mental health care can be the basis for improvements in payment systems for depression and other mental health conditions. Most importantly, it is unnecessary to expose families to risk of financial ruin in the pursuit of cost control. Arbitrary limits on inpatient coverage are an inferior form of cost containment, being dominated by supply-side payment systems methods (and possibly by managed care). Relatively 'generous' insurance coverage from the patient's point of view can be provided at a reasonable cost with the judicious combination of demand- and supply-side cost-sharing.

While noting that improvements in many plans are possible, the ability of payment changes to solve the coexisting conditions of under-treatment for some and over-treatment for others is limited. The limit is partly imposed by our limited knowledge: for example, we do not know how to pay primary care practitioners to elicit their effort to seek out depression in their practice. The limit is also due to the inherent limits of the power of payment systems as a single policy device: even if we pay primary care practitioners properly, we will not find and treat all conditions that could be treated in a cost-effective manner with the current technology of care.

Bibliography

American Psychiatric Association, Committee on Nomenclature and Statistics (1980) *Diagnostic and Statistical Manual of Mental Disorders—DSM-III*, 3rd edn. Washington, DC: APA.

American Psychiatric Association, Committee on Nomenclature and Statistics (1987) *Diagnostic and Statistical Manual of Mental Disorders—DSM-III-R,* 3rd edn, revised. Washington, DC: APA.

Andreasen NC, Grove WM, Endicott J *et al.* (1988) The phenomenology of depression. *Psychiatry and Psychobiology* **3**, 1–10.

Boyer WF and Feighner JP (1992) An overview of paraxetine. *J Clin Psychiatry* **53** (2, Suppl.), 3–6.

Broadhead WE, Blazer DG, George LK and Chiu Kit Tse (1990) Depression, disability days, and days lost from work in prospective epidemiologic survey. *JAMA* **264**, 1067–1090.

Eisenberg L (1992) Treating depression and anxiety in primary care: closing the gap between knowledge and practice. *N Engl J Med* **326**, 1080–1084.

Elkin I, Shea T, Watkins JT *et al.* (1989) National Institute of Mental Health Treatment of Depression Collaborative Research Program. *Arch Gen Psychiatry* **46**, 971–982.

Feighner JP (1985) A comparative trial of fluoxetine and amitriptyline in patients with major depressive disorder. *J Clin Psychiatry* **46**, 369–372.

Frank E, Kupfer DJ, Perel JM *et al.* (1990) Three-year outcomes for maintenance therapies in current depression. *Arch Gen Psychiatry* **47**, 1093–1099.

Frank E, Prien RF, Jarrett RB *et al.* (1991) Conceptualization and rationale for consensus definitions of terms in major depressive disorder: remission, recovery, relapse, and recurrence. *Arch Gen Psychiatry* **48**, 851–855.

Frank R, Goldman H and McGuire T (1992) A model benefit for mental health care in private insurance. *Health Affairs*, **11**, 98–117.

Goodwin FK and Jamison KR (1990) *Manic Depressive Illness.* New York: Oxford University Press.

Harrow B and Ellis R (1992) Mental health provider response to the reimbursement system. In: Frank R and Manning W (eds) *Economics and Mental Health*. Baltimore: Johns Hopkins University Press, 19–39.

Hodgkin, D. (1992) The impact of private utilization management on psychiatric care: a review of the literature. *The Journal of Mental Health Administration*, **19**, 143–157.

Horgan CM (1985) Specialty and general ambulatory mental health services: comparison of utilization and expenditures. *Arch Gen Psychiatry* **42**, 565–572.

Horgan C (1986) The demand for ambulatory mental health services from specialty providers. *Health Services Res* **21**, 291–320.

Kamlet MS, Wade M, Kupfer D, Frank E (1992) Cost-utility analysis of maintenance treatment for recurrent depression: a theoretical framework and numerical illustration. In: R Frank and W Manning (eds) *Essays in Honor of Carl Taube*. Baltimore: Johns Hopkins University Press, 267–291.

Keller MB, Klerman GL, Lavori PW *et al.* (1982) Treatment received by depressed patients. *JAMA* **248**, 1848–1856.

Keller MB, Lavori PW, Klerman GL *et al.* (1986) Low levels and lack of predictors of somatotherapy and psychotherapy received by depressed patients. *Arch Gen Psychiatry* **43**, 458–466.

Klerman GL, Weismann MM, Roundsaville BJ and Chevron ES (eds) (1984) *Interpersonal Psychotherapy of Depression*. Basic Books: New York.

Kupfer DJ (1991) Long-term treatment of depression. *J Clin Psychiatry* **52** (Suppl.), 28–34.

Leighton DC, Harding JS, Macklin DB, MacMillan AM and Leighton AH (1963) *The Character of Danger: Psychiatric Symptoms in Selected Communities*. New York: Basic Books.

Manning WG, Wells KB, Buchanan JL *et al.* (1989) Effects of mental health insurance: evidence from the health insurance experiment. *Rand Corporation Report* R-3815-NIMH/HCFA.

McGuire TG (1991) Designing a payment plan for mental health services: an application to 'company X'. Department of Economics, Boston University.

Mechanic D (1990) Treating mental illness: generalist versus specialist. *Health Affairs* **9**, 61–75.

Potter WZ, Rudorfer MV and Manji H (1991) The pharmacologic treatment of depression. *N Engl J Med* **325**, 633–642.

Robins LN, Helzer JE, Croughan J and Ratcliff KS (1981) National Institute of Mental Health Diagnostic Interview Schedule. *Arch Gen Psychiatry* **38**, 381–389.

Robins LN and Regier DA (eds) (1991) *Psychiatric Disorders in America: The Epidemiologic Catchment Area Study*. New York: Free Press.

Robins LN, Locke BZ and Regier DA (1991) An overview of psychiatric disorders in America. In: Robins LN and Regier DA (eds) *Psychiatric Disorders in America: The Epidemiologic Catchment Area Study*. New York: Free Press.

Schulberg HC, Saul M, McClelland M *et al.* (1985) Assessing depression in primary medical and psychiatric practices. *Arch Gen Psychiatry* **42**, 1164–1170.

Shapiro S, Skinner EA, Kessler LG *et al.* (1984) Utilization of health and mental health services. *Arch Gen Psychiatry* **41**, 971–978.

Srole L, Langner TS, Michael ST, Opler M and Rennie T (1962) *Mental Health in Metropolis: The Midtown Manhattan Study*. New York: McGraw-Hill.

Taube CA and Barrett SA (eds) (1985) *Mental Health, United States, 1985*, National Institute of Mental Health, DHHS Pub. No. (ADM) 85-1378. Washington, DC: US Government Printing Office.

Taube C, Burns B and Kessler L (1984) Patients of psychiatrists and psychologists in office-based practice: 1980. *Am Psychol* **39**, 1435–1447.

Taube CA, Goldman HH, Burns BJ and Kessler LG (1988) High users of outpatient mental health services, I: definitions and characteristics. *Am J Psychiatry* **145**, 19–24.

Taube C, Goldman H and Salkever D (1990) Medicaid coverage for mental illness. *Health Affairs* **9**, 5–18.

Wells KB (1985) *Depression as a Tracer Condition for the National Study of Medical Care Outcomes: Background Review*. Rand Corporation, R-3293-RWJ/HJK.

Wells KB, Manning WG Jr, Duan N, Ware J Jr and Newhouse JP (1982) *Cost Sharing and the Demand for Ambulatory Mental Health Services*. Rand Corporation, R-2960-HHS.

Wells KB, Hays RD, Burnam MA *et al.* (1989a) Detection of depressive disorder for patients receiving prepaid or fee-for-service care. *JAMA* **262**, 3298–3302.
Wells KB, Stewart A, Hays RD *et al.* (1989b) The functioning and well-being of depressed patients. *JAMA* **262**, 914–919.
Wells KB, Manning WG and Valdez RB (1989c) The effects of insurance generosity on the psychological distress and well-being of a general population. Rand Corporation, R-3682-NIMH/HCFA, Santa Monica, CA.

7

The economic impact of an educational programme on diagnosis and treatment of depression in Sweden

Jan Wålinder, Per Carlsson and Wolfgang Rutz

Introduction

Clinical depression: a common disease

Clinical depression is said to be the commonest emotional disorder, affecting about 50% of North Americans and Western Europeans at some time in their lives (Editorial, 1992a). It has been estimated that the prevalence of depressed patients in need of medical care is in the range of 3–5% of the population (Hagnell, 1990). According to reports by Rutz (1992) and West (1992) depressive disorders are under-recognized and therefore under-treated. Only a small proportion of patients reach a psychiatrist and are given adequate treatment and follow-up. This leads to subjective suffering as well as increased sick-leave and consumption of medical care. The suicide rate in severely melancholic patients approximates 15% and some 2000 suicides are committed each year in Sweden. The annual incidence of suicide per 100 000 inhabitants in Sweden is 34.8 for males and 14.8 for females and exceeds that of many malignant diseases. Since 1970 the age-adjusted suicide rate has shown a slight downward trend for men. The rate for women has been stable over the last 20 years (Socialstyrelsen, 1991).

It is estimated that 40–50% of all suicides are committed by patients with undiagnosed or inadequately treated depressive disorders (Avery and Winokur, 1976; Rhimer *et al.*, 1990; Paykel, 1991). Even higher figures have been

Health Economics of Depression. Edited by B. Jönsson and J. Rosenbaum
© 1993 John Wiley & Sons Ltd.

presented. Thus it is mentioned that 70% of the 4000 people who commit suicide each year in the UK are thought to have had a depressive disorder (Editorial, 1992a). Epidemiological and family studies show an increase in the rates of major depression between 1960 and 1975 in several countries including Sweden (Klerman and Weissman, 1989).

Depression also has substantial socioeconomic consequences. The costs for depression in the United States has been estimated at 29 billion dollars (Abraham *et al.*, 1991). The indirect costs included 18 billion dollars for absenteeism, and 6 billion dollars for mortality as a consequence of suicide. The direct costs for treatment represented 14% of the total costs. This relation indicates that rather small improvements in prevention or treatment of depression could lead to a significant reduction of the total costs for the disease in society.

There is evidence that maintenance treatment could be effective and that careful long-term treatment can decrease the suicide rate for patients with mood disorder (Editorial, 1992b). Still, there are very few evaluations of programmes for prevention, and the number of economic evaluations is even fewer. In order to assess the costs and benefits of an educational strategy for prevention of suicide and depression morbidity a study was set up on the Swedish island of Gotland, which has a well-defined and stable population. The initiative for the project was provided by the Swedish Committee for Prevention and Treatment of Depression (the Swedish PTD Committee). The purpose of the educational programme, which was conducted between 1983 and 1984, was to improve the knowledge among general practitioners (GPs) concerning diagnoses and treatment of depression.

Evaluation of prevention
During recent decades, increasing attention has been paid to postgraduate medical training throughout the world. Large amounts of effort and money are spent in postgraduate training, but still very little is known about the effects of the educational programmes. Student opinion is not systematically used in the evaluation of psychiatric teaching (Perris, 1972), and even less is known about the effects of the programmes on the health care system (Berg, 1979). In one of the very few trials of the effects of continuing medical education the results were not encouraging (Siebley *et al.*, 1982). There was little effect on the overall quality of care. Thus systematic evaluations of educational efforts are very much needed.

The Swedish PTD Committee hypothesized that a favourable outcome of the training project would lead to changes in the utilization of medical care at the local psychiatric department, reduced sick-leave frequencies due to depressive disorders and a changed prescription pattern for psychopharmaceutical drugs. A number of items which would illustrate such changes were chosen for a follow-up of the educational programme. It was feared that increased primary care involvement in the treatment of depressive disorders might lead to an increased risk of suicide. For that reason the suicide rate was also observed, so that a possible increase would be identified at an early stage.

An economic evaluation was linked to the programme in order to determine whether or not the costs of the training programme would be counterbalanced by positive savings and benefits to the health service and to society as a whole.

It has been considered that psychiatry is difficult to analyse economically (Rutz, 1992; World Health Organization Scientific Group Report, 1991). One important reason is the lack of tradition in psychiatric care to conduct trials to establish the effectiveness of new methods. This is partly understood by the fact that the treatment is often individualized for every patient and it is difficult to define and compare different methods. However, when the effectiveness of a defined method is established – it may be difficult to transform the effects into economic terms of the same size as in other health care sectors.

Economic evaluation
The identification, quantification and evaluation of relevant costs for diagnosis and treatment in psychiatric care are similar to the way costs are estimated in other fields, e.g. surgery or internal medicine. However, in one respect it may be more complicated to measure all relevant costs in psychiatric care compared with other fields of medicine, since the treatment of mental disorders often includes social care and other services outside the health care sector. In general the accounting systems in the social sector are less developed than comparable systems in health care. This makes it virtually impossible to find accurate cost information.

When hospital care in general becomes more outpatient oriented (e.g. day surgery and the growing integration between hospital care and home care), the methodological problems in quantifying the total costs for an episode of treatment become similar for surgical patients and for psychiatric patients.

A remaining difference between psychiatric care and other sectors is the ability to get accurate answers from patients involved in evaluation of effects of the treatment on quality of life or functioning status. In general, evaluations in psychiatric care have to rely relatively more heavily on observations by professionals or family members, compared with evaluations in other sectors. Changes in patients' health status are often studied by means of health indicators (e.g. return to work, ability to live outside institutions) rather than by more objective measures of health.

There are several optional methods for economic evaluations in health care. All of them can be adequate for studies in psychiatric care. The choice of method depends on the problem studied and the availability of relevant data. A cost-of-illness approach provides an estimate of the costs of burden of different diseases but does not indicate the best way to reduce such costs or improve health. Cost-of-illness studies in psychiatry could be of great value when they are used as a frame of reference for allocation of resources, e.g. to research and technology assessment.

A real economic evaluation is designed to compare two or more alternative methods or programmes. Cost-effectiveness analyses include comparisons of both costs and effects for at least two alternatives. The net costs in society for each option are related to a primary effect variable, e.g. number of successfully treated patients or number of days without pain. This type of analysis could be useful in the evaluation of psychiatric care but often the treatment objective is complex, and a number of effects should be considered. When both improvements in the length and quality of life should be considered, cost-utility analysis may be superior to cost-effectiveness analysis. One limitation with the application of cost-utility analysis in psychiatric care is the obvious difficulties in involving patients in the valuation of utilities of relevant health states.

The result of cost-effectiveness and cost-utility analysis may be a helpful guide for decision-makers in the allocation of resources within a defined budget. In that respect the cost–benefit approach (CBA) is different. Both costs and outcomes are evaluated in monetary terms, allowing judgements to be made between programmes in several sectors of society. The CBA method also makes it possible to restrict the evaluation to a single alternative, which is often the case when educational programmes are to be evaluated. The main disadvantage with this approach is the focusing on monetary valuation of certain important aspects of clinical outcome. Difficulties in translating pain and suffering into monetary terms sometimes lead to failure to consider these aspects, which could lead to over- or underestimation of the total benefit of the programme. Despite these problems we found CBA to be the most adequate method in this study.

Description of the educational programme

The island of Gotland forms a psychiatric catchment area of 56 000 inhabitants. There is one psychiatric department on the island, and at the time the project was carried out 18 general practitioners were working there. In 1983 and 1984 all GPs were invited to participate in two two-day courses on the diagnoses and treatment of depression. The training was given by the Swedish PTD group.

Course I
Each course was given twice, as it was impossible to gather all the island's GPs on the same occasion. The two-day course included the following lectures:

- Classification of depressive disorders.
- Aetiology and pathogenesis of depressive disorders.
- The treatment of the depressed patient.
- Depression in old age.
- Treatment practice for depression on Gotland.
- Long-term treatment and prophylaxis for depressive disorders.

- Discussion of case reports.

Course II

In the second programme, the committee tried to include a series of topics requested by the general practitioners in the evaluation after the first educational programme. The topics covered were:

- Depressive disorders in childhood and adolescence.
- Suicidology.
- Psychotherapy.
- The depressed patient and his family.
- Discussion of case reports.

Some 90% of all permanently employed GPs took part in the training programme.

Study design

Effects of the programme

The year before the educational programme was launched was chosen as the baseline year. The following variables were recorded: sick-leave due to depressive disorders on Gotland, emergency case patterns and consumption of inpatient psychiatric care, prescription of drugs relevant to the treatment of depression, the suicide rate on Gotland and the suicidants' contacts with the primary care and psychiatric care sectors, respectively. The programme was basically evaluated through 1985 with regard to the above-mentioned items. During an extended follow-up period from 1986 to 1988 effects of time were especially studied with regard to the suicide rate, utilization of inpatient care and prescription of psychopharmaceutical drugs. It was assumed that the programme did not result in any quantitative changes in the primary care of depressed patients.

The study design is shown in Figure 1.

Baseline	*October 1982*
Control period I	October 1982–January 1983
Inquiry 1	February 1983
First PTD educational programme	April–May 1983
Control period II	October 1983–January 1984
Inquiry 2	April 1984
Second PTD educational programme	June–August 1984
Control period III	October 1984–January 1985
Inquiry 3	March 1985
Control period IV	October 1985–January 1986
Control period V	October–December 1988

Figure 1   Study design

Calculation of costs and benefits

What kind of costs should be included in the economic evaluation? In this study the intervention costs were important. They consisted of the preparation costs for the educational programme, the costs of executing the programme, and the costs resulting from the loss of ordinary production for the teachers and for the doctors who participated in the programme. The salary per day including payroll taxes was taken as an approximate measure of the production loss in the respective groups. The cost estimates were supplemented using data from the Municipality of Gotland on average salaries for GPs (including tax costs) and the total expenses incurred by the Swedish PTD Committee, including loss of production as above.

It was assumed that the prescription level for drugs would have been the same during the baseline year if the programme had not been started. The cost increase for antidepressant drugs was calculated on the basis of the prescription during the baseline year 1982, compared with the amount of daily doses (DDD) of antidepressants prescribed during the follow-up years 1983, 1984 and 1985.

All cost estimates were based on the measure of a defined daily dose per 1000 inhabitants per day and were transformed to the annual consumption and related to the population of Gotland (see Table 1).

Table I. Comparison of drug costs, based on number of prescriptions, betweeen the baseline year, 1982, and the short-term follow-up years 1983–1985. Cost of a defined daily dose (DDD) calculated from the average price for the three most common drugs used. From Rutz *et al.*, (1992a), with permission. © 1992 Munksgaard International Publishers Ltd, Copenhagen, Denmark.

	Mean drug use: (DDD per 1000 inhabitants per day)				Difference in cost (SEK) (DDD/1000 inh./day × cost/
	Baseline 1982	Follow-up 1983–1985	Change between baseline and follow-up	Mean cost per DDD (SEK/DDD)	DDD × 365 days × 3 years × number of inh.)
Antidepressants	3.9	5.2	+1.3	3.03	+242 000
Major tranquillizers	11.6	9.7	−1.9	2.98	−347 000
Day sedatives	16.8	15.6	−1.2	1.66	−122 000
Night sedatives	34.6	34.6	0	0.81	0
Lithium	1.5	1.5	0	1.40	0
Tota drug consumption; net cost reduction					227 000

The savings resulting from reduced inpatient care of patients with depressive disorders were calculated on the basis of the average costs per day at the Department of Psychiatry. The annual consumption of inpatient care was calculated on the last quarter of each of the years in the follow-up period.

Calculation of savings from indirect effects of the programme on sick-leave and reduced mortality is controversial in many respects. This reflects most of the problems concerning calculation of indirect costs discussed in textbooks on health economics (McGuire *et al.*, 1988). For practical reasons, we choose a human capital approach. It prescribes that the value of life of an individual is equal to the present value of future lost output, e.g. labour costs. A calculation of the production gains as an approximation of the benefit from reduction in morbidity and mortality has weaknesses. One is the underestimation of the value of health improvements among unemployed and retired. Another is valuation of the costs for the production losses. Is the average salary plus pay-roll taxes an acceptable approximation for short-term and long-term sick-leave? The calculation of the savings due to the observed positive trend in the sick-leave statistics takes no account of the so-called 'intangible effects' such as 'quality of life'.

Our estimation is based on the National Insurance Office's calculations of the costs of a day's sick-leave for the normal population, postulating that the depressed patient does not differ from the average person in this respect. Age distribution and employment rate support this assumption. With this method of calculation, we used sickness benefit as an approximate measure of the loss in production. This estimate is obviously rather rough and probably too low rather than too high.

In this study the costs and savings during the period in which the programme was carried out have been calculated on the basis of the value of the Swedish crown (SEK) in 1988. We used the Swedish Social Insurance Office's conversion table. During the study period 1982–1988 the price increased by 45%.

Sensitivity analyses

The number of suicides can either be based on figures reported by the police authorities on Gotland or the National Statistics Office of Sweden (SCB). The figures provided by the police are a direct reflection of completed suicides on Gotland, while the SCB figures include suicides committed elsewhere in Sweden by persons who are census registered on Gotland. For this reason, we considered the police figures to be more valid. However, we have made estimates based on both data sources.

The number of years saved for each individual case of prevented suicide was estimated by calculating the value of lives saved using the statistical model employed by the Traffic Safety Board. In 1988 they estimated the value of a saved life to be SEK 7.4 million regardless of age (see Persson, 1991). A sensitivity analysis of the calculation of the reduced costs due to saved lives was conducted by using alternative figures for the value per saved life.

Results

The costs for the educational programme were estimated to SEK 369 000 (Table II). Regarding the prescription of drugs it changed to a more adequate prescription pattern of antidepressants and reduced consumption of daytime and nighttime sedatives. The daily doses of prescribed antidepressant drugs were found to have increased during the evaluation period, giving an additional cost of SEK 242 000. Changes in the pattern of prescribed daytime sedatives, hypnotics and major tranquillizers resulted in a drug cost reduction of SEK 469 000. That means that a net cost reduction in relation to the total drug consumption was SEK 227 000 (Tables I and (II).

The estimated saving of days in inpatient care resulted in a reduction of costs by SEK 11.25 million (Table II). Regarding morbidity we noted a sick-leave reduction which translates into a saving of approximately SEK 3.4 million as a measure of the reduction in loss of production (Table II).

When looking at mortality, the expected number of suicides during the evaluation period was calculated to be 39. The actual number during the period was 20, giving an assumed number of prevented suicides of 19. Using the Traffic Safety Board's model as the basis of calculation this resulted in savings to society of SEK 140.6 million (Tables II and III).

All these changes contrast with previous trends on Gotland, concomitant

Table II. Cost–benefit analysis of an educational programme for GPs on Gotland. From Rutz *et al.*, (1992a), with permission. © 1992 Munksgaard International Publishers Ltd, Copenhagen, Denmark.

Direct costs 'Intervention' (SEK)		Direct costs 'Process' (SEK)		Indirect costs 'Outcome' (SEK)	
Educational programme	+212 000	*Drugs* Antidepressants	+242 000	*Morbidity* Days on sick-leave	−3 400 000
		Major tranquillizers	−347 000		
		Day sedatives	−122 000		
Drop in production: GPs	+80 000	Night sedatives	±0		
		Net	−227 000	*Mortality* Numbers of suicides	−140 600 000
		Outpatient care	±0		
Drop in production: teachers, PTD Committee	+77 000	*Inpatient care* Reduction in costs due to reduced hospitalization	−11 250 000		
Total	+369 000	Total	−11 477 000	Total	−144 000 000
Net gain approximately = 155 000 000 SEK					

Table III. The financial benefits of a reduced number of suicides, based on three calculations of the value of a human life. From Rutz *et al.*, (1992a), with permission. © 1992 Munksgaard International Publishers Ltd, Copenhagen, Denmark.

Reduced number of suicides	Benefit of an avoidable death		
	2.5 million SEK[a]	7.4 million SEK[b]	15 million SEK[c]
Reported by the police *n* = 19	SEK 47.5	SEK 140.6	SEK 285
According the the Central Bureau of Statistics *n* = 7	SEK 17.5	SEK 51.8	SEK 105

[a] Estimated savings of years lost according to valuation recommended by the National Board of Health and Welfare (Socialstyrelsen, 1991).
[b] Value of a life according to the Traffic Safety Board 1988 (Vägverket, 1986).
[c] Value of a life according to the expert group on Traffic Safety 1990 (Expertgruppen för trafiksäkerhet, 1991).

trends in Sweden as a whole and a previous observed parallelism between trends in Gotland and in the country as a whole (Rutz, 1992). A time effect was also noted for these changes in so far that the positive effects vanished over time and approached baseline values.

In summary the total cost of the Swedish PTD programme of approximately SEK 369 000 was counterbalanced by total savings of approximately SEK 155 million during the three-year evaluation period of the programme (Table II). Even when the low figures of prevented suicides and savings per prevented suicide where used the total savings were counterbalanced by the costs for the educational programme.

Discussion

The lack of systematic cost–benefit studies in public health care is a well-known problem. The purpose of this study was to investigate whether or not and to what extent the educational programme could result in gains to society. Although the basis of our calculations is open to debate, it is obvious that the programme has resulted in a benefit far greater than the costs for the educational programme.

This study illustrates many of the methodological difficulties connected with evaluations of programmes in health care in general and in psychiatry specifically. However, it also shows the existing opportunities for performing systematic evaluations on effects and costs of programmes in psychiatric care.

As previously stated, an evaluation of the effects of an educational programme on the health care system has to use a quasi-experimental design (Campbell, 1984). However, there is a risk of misinterpreting the trends unrelated to the educational programmes as real effects (Ottosson, 1984). One such example is the interpretation of the effect of the Samaritans' contact programme on suicide prevention in England, where a decline in suicide rate was later found to be related to a decrease in the content of carbon monoxide in household gas and not to the contact programme as such (Jennings *et al.*, 1978; Kreitman, 1980). In the present series of studies (Eberhard *et al.*, 1986; Rutz *et al.*, 1989a, 1989b; Rutz, 1990) the effects within the study area (Gotland) have been carefully observed in comparison with general trends in Sweden as a whole.

The question why we did not immediately offer the GPs continued training when beneficial effects were noted may of course be asked. However, from a scientific point of view, we considered an evaluation with a sufficiently long observation period important in order to detect effects, if any, which could be interpreted as signs of the specific effect of the programme. In this study of the long-term effects we noted that the effects were strictly related in time to the educational programmes. In 1985, all the effects were at their peaks, and later on the effects declined (Rutz *et al.*, 1992*b*).

Thus, it seems justified to conclude that the educational programme given to the GPs on Gotland had significantly affected many important areas of the health care system. The frequency of sick-leave and of inpatient care for depressive disorders decreased, the patterns of prescription of psychotropic drugs changed and the frequency of suicide decreased. However, the effects of the educational programme did not last long. If long-term effects are to be achieved it seems obvious that educational programmes have to be repeated about every second to third year.

In the cost–benefit analysis our calculations are generally based on rough estimates. This was made with the knowledge that any attempt to make detailed calculations would only result in increased pseudo-precision. Nor would they improve the possibility of judging the economic benefits of projects of this kind.

The calculation of the savings to society as a result of the Swedish PTD programme is affected above all by the method of estimating the monetary value of prevented suicides and saved adult human lives. As an alternative to the Traffic Safety Board's price, we have calculated the value of the prevented suicides on Gotland on the basis of the average age of suicide victims on Gotland during the Swedish PTD programme evaluation period (46 years), the mean life expectancy (79 years) and the National Board of Health and Welfare's recommendations to the National Health Service regarding the value of one saved year of life (Socialstyrelsen, 1991). If this method of calculation is applied, a prevented suicide on Gotland results in savings of SEK 2 500 000 and the total number of saved years during the evaluation period would correspond to approximately SEK 47 000 000. Yet another alternative to the Traffic Safety Board's price of SEK 7 400 000 of a saved human life is the recommendation made by the Expert Group on Traffic Safety in 1990 that this amount should be increased to about SEK 15 000 000 per death (Expertgruppen för trafiksäkerhet, 1991). Our presentation is based on suicides reported by the local police authority. This seems to be the most realistic reporting from a local perspective and has also been used in a previous study.

There are small uncertainties as regards the costs of the actual educational programme. Concerning the calculation of the costs of the drugs it may be questioned whether the decreased prescribing of major tranquillizers is solely an effect of the Swedish PTD programme. Changes in the general attitude towards the treatment of schizophrenic syndromes may have played a role in this context. We do, however, believe that the reduced prescription of major tranquillizers as daytime and night-time sedatives can be ascribed to the educational programme. However, if we disregard the changes in the prescription of major tranquillizers the net saving in drug costs of about SEK 227 000 changes to an increase in drug costs of about SEK 120 000. However, this does not substantially affect the total result of the study.

During the evaluation period a reduction in sick-leave frequency could be observed only in patients suffering from depressive syndromes. The amount of sick-leave for other medical reasons remained the same during the period. The observed sick-leave reduction only applies to the working population. If a person with a disability pension recovers from his or her depressive illness, this will not be reflected by the statistics. This benefit should be considered as being part of the non-monetary 'intangible effects', such as improved quality of life or the value of not being sick.

In order to study the effects of intervention at a societal level, non-experimental studies and secondary data from available records generally compiled for other purposes are often the only options (Carlsson, 1987). We have used data on number of suicides from two sources in order to validate the number reported by the police. There were differences in number of suicides but the direction of the change was the same.

Human suffering can be reduced if depressed patients are handled and cared for in a professional manner. Compared to other health service interventions, where the health service often has to make major investments in order to achieve savings to the national economy, educational programmes of the kind discussed here are effective as the intervention costs are low in relation to the monetary savings made and other benefits gained. The effect levels off over time and the educational programme should therefore be repeated approximately every second or third year.

In our study we failed to capture the so-called 'intangible effects'. It may seem natural that the quality of life in depressed or suicidal persons would be much lower compared with an average individual. However, everyday clinical experience points to the contrary, namely that persons who have been successfully treated for a depressive disorder perform very well and manage to achieve a high quality of life.

The national health policies in Sweden and abroad indicate that an increasing proportion of the health service's responsibility and resources will be transferred to primary health care. This means the need for high-quality assurance and standards of medical knowledge within primary health care. For the future, this makes the kind of postgraduate training offered by the Swedish PTD committee even more important. The study also shows the need for systematic evaluations including economic consequences in order to support the continuation of the programme and diffusion of ideas to other populations inside and outside Sweden.

Acknowledgements

This chapter is primarily based on the paper by W. Rutz, P. Carlsson, L. von Knorring and J. Wålinder (1992), 'Cost–benefit analysis of an educational program for general practitioners by the Swedish Committee for the prevention and treatment of depression', published in *Acta Psychiatrica Scandinavica*, **85**, 457–464; von Knorring, Rutz and Wålinder are members of the Swedish PTD Committee.

We would like to thank the other members of the Swedish PTD Commitee: Professor Göran Eberhard, Professor Gunnar Holmberg, Professor Anne-Liis von Knorring, Assistant Professor Börje Wistedt and Assistant Professor Anna Åberg-Wistedt.

Mr Gunnar Dahlgren at the Ciba-Geigy Pharmaceutical Division, Västra Frölunda, Sweden, is acknowledged for important support and help in technical and administrative matters.

Her Majesty Queen Silvia of Sweden is patron to the Swedish PTD Committee.

References

Abraham IL, Neese JB and Westerman JB (1991) Depression. *Nurs Clin North Am* **26**, 527–544.

Avery D and Winokur G (1976) Mortality in depressed patients treated with electroconvulsive therapy and antidepressants. *Arch Gen Psychiatry* **33**, pp. 1029–1037.

Berg AD (1979) Does continuing medical education improve quality of medical care? A look at evidence. *J Fam Pract* **8**, 1171–1174.

Campbell DT (1984) Hospital and Landsting as continuously monitoring social polygrams: advocacy and warning. In: Cronholm C *et al.* (eds) *Evaluation of mental health services programs*. Stockholm: Swedish Medical Research Council, pp. 13–39.

Carlsson P (1987) Spridning och ekonomiska effekter av medicinsk teknologi. Linköping. *Stud Arts Sci* no. 12.

Eberhard G, Holmberg G, von Knorring A-L, von Knorring L, Rutz W, Wistedt B, Wålinder J. and Åberg-Wistedt A (1986) Evaluation of postgraduate medical education given by the Swedish PTD Committee. *Nord Psychiat Tidsskr* **40**, 185–192.

Editorial (1992a) Iceberg of depression. *Lancet* **339**, 985.

Editorial (1992b) Depression and suicide: are they preventable?, *Lancet* **340**, 700–701.

Expertgruppen för trafiksäkerhet (1991) *Samhällsekonomisk prioritering av trafik-säkerhetsåtgärder.* Huvudrapport 1991.

Hagnell O (1990) *The incidence of mental illness over a quarter of a century. The Lundby longitudinal study of mental illness in a total population based on 42.000 observation years.* Stockholm: Almkvist & Wiksell.

Jennings C, Barraclough BM and Moss JR (1978) Have the Samaritans lowered the suicidal rate? *Psychol Med* **18**, 413–422.

Klerman GL and Weissman MM (1989) Increasing rates of depression. *JAMA* **261**, 2229–2235.

Krietman N (1980) Die Epidemiologie von Suizid und Parasuizid. *Nervenarzt* **51**, 131–138.

McGuire A, Henderson J and Mooney G (1988) *The Economics of Health Care: An Introductory Text.* London: Routledge & Kegan Paul.

Ottosson JO (1984) Introduction to general discussion. In: Cronholm C *et al.* (eds) *Evaluation of mental health services programs.* Stockholm: Swedish Medical Research Council. pp. 180–199.

Paykel ES (1991) Epidemiology and prognosis of depression. In: Racagni G *et al.* (eds) *Biological Psychiatry,* Vol. 1, pp. 57–60. Amsterdam: Elsevier Science Publishers.

Perris C (1972) The use of student opinion in the evaluation of undergraduate psychiatric training. *Arch Psicol Neurol Psichiat (Milano)* **1**, 121–130.

Persson, U (1991) Priset för ett människoliv—7,4 miljoner kronor—styr vägbyggandet, *Stadsbyggnad* **1**, 11–13.

Rhimer Z, Barsi J, Veg K and Katona C (1990) Suicide rates in Hungary correlate negatively with reported rates of depression. *J Affective Disord* **20**, 87–91.

Rutz W, Wålinder J, Eberhard G, Holmberg G, von Knorring A-L, von Knorring L, Wistedt B and Åberg-Wistedt A (1989a) An educational program on depressive disorders for general practitioners on Gotland: background and evaluation. *Acta Psychiatr Scand* **79**, 19–26.

Rutz W, von Knorring L and Wålinder J (1989b) Frequency of suicide on Gotland after systematic postgraduate education of general practitioners. *Acta Psychiatr Scand* **80**, 151–154.

Rutz W, von Knorring L, Wålinder J and Wistedt B (1990) Effect of an educational program for general practitioners on Gotland on the pattern of prescription of psychotropic drugs. *Acta Psychiatr Scand* **82**, 399–403.

Rutz W (1992) Evaluation of an educational program on depressive disorders given to general practitioners on Gotland. Short- and long-term effects. *Linköping University Medical Dissertations,* No. 356.

Rutz W, Carlsson P, von Knorring L and Wålinder J (1992a) Cost–benefit analysis of an educational program for general practitioners by the Swedish Committee for Prevention and Treatment of Depression. *Acta Psychiatr Scand,* **85**, 457–464.

Rutz W, von Knorring L and Wålinder J (1992b) Long-term effects of an educational program for general practitioners given by the Swedish Committee for the Prevention and Treatment of Depression. *Acta Psychiatr Scand* **85**, 83–88.

Siebley JC, Sachett DL, Neufeld V, Gerrard B, Rudmik KV and Fraser W (1982) A randomized trial of continuing education. *N Engl J Med* **37**, 383–388.
Socialstyrelsen (1991) Folkhälsorapport 1991. Stockholm. *SoS-rapport* **1991**, 11.
Vägverket (1986) *Serviceavdelningen: Planering och projektering*. Vägverkets publikationer 1986, 6.
West R (1992) *Depression*. London: Office of Health Economics.
World Health Organization (1991) Evaluation of methods for the treatment of mental disorders. Report of a WHO Scientific Group, *WHO Technical Report Series* 812, Geneva.

8

The challenge of measuring quality of life in psychiatric patients

P. Bech, G.C. Dunbar and M.J. Stoker

Introduction

This chapter is presented in two parts. The first addresses some general issues obtained following a review of recent developments in quality of life (QOL) scales. The second describes, in detail, a specific scale designed to measure QOL change in non-psychotic psychiatric patients—SBQOL.

Recent developments in QOL assessment

Clinical disability and health-related QOL

In clinical psychiatry it is often difficult to distinguish sharply between diseases which make the person ill and other states of health which do not cause illness, but which make the person uncomfortable and distressed. The International Classification of Impairments, Disabilities and Handicaps (World Health Organization (WHO), 1980) was a major attempt to develop both a language with strict clinical referents (covering impairments and disabilities) and a less clinical language (covering handicaps).

According to WHO (1980) impairments refer to the biological abnormalities of the disease under study, whereas disabilities refer to the clinical symptoms of that disease. Disability is often described by symptoms of behaviour or performance.

Health Economics of Depression. Edited by B. Jönsson and J. Rosenbaum
© 1993 John Wiley & Sons Ltd.

In research on depressive disorders, the introduction of selective serotonin reuptake inhibitors (SSRIs), e.g. Feighner and Boyer (1991), has had significant impact on our understanding of depressive disorders. Serotonin must play a major role in the impairment of depression because the new SSRI drugs (citalopram, fluvoxamine, fluoxetine, paroxetine and sertraline), significantly reduce the clinical disability of depressed patients. In the various controlled studies with these compounds (Feighner and Boyer, 1991), the Hamilton Depression Rating Scale (HAM-D) (Hamilton, 1967) has been used to measure change in depressed patients' disability.

In pharmo-economic research, outcomes of drug therapy can be divided (Chrischilles, 1992), into 'raw' health effects, QOL and economic consequences. Within the WHO frame of reference, handicap is equated with QOL. Handicap, according to WHO (1980), covers the subjective disadvantage experienced by the patient as a result of the impairment and disability caused by disease. Raw health measures in psychiatric patients included symptomatic scales such as the HAM-D.

The essential aspect of health-related QOL is to help the patient to communicate the extent to which the present illness influences his or her personal life. In this context Joyce (1992) has defined health-related QOL as 'what the patient says it is'. However, insight in psychiatric patients includes self-knowledge both about how the disorder affects self and about how the disorder affects their interaction with the world. In patients with dementia and schizophrenia, insight is poor or even absent. In such cases it is important to take the care-giver's perceived burden into account, e.g. by use of Caregiver Hassles Scale (Kinney and Stephens,1989). Considerations of insight clearly imply limitations in the use of self-rating scales in dementia and schizophrenia, but also in major depression, at least during the first weeks of treatment.

Instruments to measure change in depression in short-term studies
Self-rating scales have been applied very little when measuring the antidepressive properties of the SSRIs. Thus no self-rating scales were used in controlled studies on citalopram and only very few in the fluvoxamine studies (Bech, 1989). A similar observation was made by Feighner and Boyer (1991) for fluoxetine, paroxetine and sertraline.

It seems that, in short-term studies, the recommendations of Hamilton (1977) have been followed: 'Clinical trials should be conducted in such a way that they resemble ordinary clinical practice as much as possible. This is one of the reasons why I have some antipathy to self-rating scales. In ordinary clinical practice a patient expects to see his physician fairly frequently, and it is the latter who ascertains the changes in a patient's condition by asking him questions and receiving replies thereto. Observer rating scales fit in very well with this procedure; self-rating scales provide an excellent excuse for the investigator to avoid interviewing his patient.'

In the short-term studies with fluvoxamine, fluoxetine and paroxetine (Bech, 1989; Feighner and Boyer, 1991), the HAM-D was found to be more sensitive in measuring change in depressive disability than self-rating scales such as the Beck Depression Inventory, the Zung Depression Scale or the Hopkins Symptom Checklist. This is consistent with the results of other studies comparing self-rating scales for depression with the Hamilton Depression Scale in short-term studies (e.g. Angst *et al.*, 1992; Edwards *et al.*, 1984).

Content validity of QOL instruments in long-term studies

QOL measurements are of particular value in the context of long-term treatment (Bech, 1993). Depressive disorders are chronic disorders, and their long-term treatment is therefore extremely important (Montgomery and Rouillon, 1992). QOL measurements in this setting cover both a separate dimension of handicap and a multidimensional approach to the assessment of improvement due to treatment.

In Table I is shown the multidimensional approach to health adopted by DSM-III (American Psychiatric Association, 1980) as well as the WHO levels of diagnosis, disability and handicap (subjective QOL). The PCASEE repertoire is based on a consensus (Walker and Asscher, 1987), including physical, cognitive, affective, social and economic QOL (PCASE). By adding another E to include ego strength or personality function (PCASEE) the correspondence to the DSM-III axes become apparent (Bech, 1987).

Table I. DSM–III multi-axial system and the PCASEE repertoire.

WHO levels of diagnosis, disability and quality of life	P = Physical (axis 3)	C = Cognitive (axis 1)	A = Affective (axis 1)	S = Social (axis 5)	E = Economic stressors (axis 5)	E = Ego functions (axis 2)
Diagnosis or syndromes	Somatic disorders	Organic brain disorders or schizophrenia	Affective disorders	Activity of daily life	Psycho-social pressures	Personality disorders
Disability or health indicators	Tiredness, sleep, appetite	Concentration, memory	Melancholia, anxiety, phobia	Group-directed behaviour, time structure	Stress behaviour	Self-identity, self-acceptance
Subjective quality of life	Good health	Decision-making good	Good emotional contact, interests	Doing things well	Feeling economic basis good	Playing useful part in things

In terms of WHO levels, instruments measuring clinical disability include such scales as the HAM-D or the Hamilton Anxiety Scale (HAMA) (Bech and Coppen, 1990). Health-related QOL scales should include both the PCASEE repertoire and how the patients perceive these dimensions.

Nomothetic and generic scales

The individual aspect of QOL was emphasized by Eysenck (1991), who throughout his scientific work has constructed scales for groups (reliable across patients; nomothetic scales). He wrote in his autobiography 'in writing one's autobiography, one inevitably has to take the idiographic pattern of trying to see regularities in one's own life, look for behaviour patterns that repeat themselves and try to discover variables that are important for oneself, even though they might not be of general interest'.

This individual aspect of QOL has not been adequately covered by the traditional self-rating scales, such as the General Health Questionnaire (Goldberg, 1972), Hopkins Sympton Checklist—SCL-90 (Guy, 1976)—or Psychological General Well-being Scale (Dupuy, 1984; Croog et al., 1986).

These traditional scales imply that QOL means the same thing to every patient (nomothetic scales). Even when such scales are applied to patients with the same disorder (disease-specific scales) the patients under examination are unlikely to come from the same population as those for whom the instrument was originally developed.

The General Health Questionnaire and the Psychological General Well-being Scale were developed as generic scales (to be used across different disorders). However, when applied to patients with depressive disorders, the following 10 items of the Psychological General Well-being Scale are disability terms rather than indicators of QOL: pains, depressed, nervous, low energy, downhearted, tense, sad, anxious, keyed-up, exhausted.

In a large study (Hunt and McKenna, 1992) on patients with depressive disorders ($N = 223$), the Psychological General Well-being Scale was compared with a disability scale for depression—the Montgomery Asberg Depression Rating Scale. The correlation between the two scales in this short-term trial was 0.49 at baseline, 0.60 after three weeks of treatment and 0.76 after six weeks of treatment. The discrimination of the two scales in terms of treatment outcome was not considered in this study.

In long-term trials with antidepressants, the Psychological General Well-being Scale seems more applicable than other generic self-rating scales because its items have bipolar definitions. Thus the item 'How satisfied have you been with your personal life?' has the following response categories: extremely happy, very happy most of the time, generally satisfied, sometimes fairly unhappy, generally dissatisfied, very dissatisfied most of the time. In long-term trials of antidepressants typically, only degrees of discomfort, not of comfort, are measured. Correlation coefficients from long-term studies are similar to results with depressed patients in short-term trials, indicating a convergence between self-rating scales and observer rating scales at the end of the trial.

Unfortunately, Hunt and McKenna (1992) have changed the item anchoring of the Psychological General Well-being Scale from the original six response categories to five alternatives. By shortening the item categories to five alternatives, it is very difficult to compare results across studies. The unique property of the Psychological General Well-being Scale is that it provides a standard of QOL in the general population, i.e. in non-patients. Normative data are available for 1209 residents in Ohio, USA. Thus the scale values of psychiatric patients can be compared directly with those for the general population, for both the total score and individual subscales.

This scale seems to be the most interesting scale among self-rating instruments to measure patients' well-being. It is short (22 items), and simple to complete. Its further merits are that the items measure frequency of symptoms rather than intensity (thereby differing from depression scales), and there are both positive and negative response alternatives (unlike most depression scales, which have only negative alternatives), thereby providing a continuum for sensitivity to change. The Psychological General Well-being Scale has, in fact, proven to be more sensitive than other group-orientated self-rating scales in patients with mild to moderate hypotension (Croog *et al.*, 1986).

This bipolar approach to response alternatives (e.g. 'How satisfied have you been with your personal life?—extremely happy; very happy most of the time; generally satisfied; sometimes fairly unhappy; generally dissatisfied; very dissatisfied most of the time') also takes into account the distance between the current state and the state the patient aims at, i.e. his or her ideal self.

Recently, an attempt to develop a disease-specific but nomothetic scale for depression has been published (Tuynman-Qua *et al.*, 1992). This scale, the Quality of Life in Depression, was found to have the same correlation with the HAM-D and the Montgomery Asberg Scale as the Psychological General Well-being Scale. Evidence of the discriminant validity of the Quality of Life in Depression Scale in long-term studies is lacking.

Idiographic and disease-specific scales

The idiographic approach to QOL assessment has, to date, been represented most adequately by the Repertory Grid Interview. This method is based on the work of Kelly (1955), who found that the best description of individual psychological processes is obtained by examining how a person constructs the world, organizing events, concepts or even other people.

By use of Kelly's approach to individual psychology, patients are helped to design their own QOL scale within the PCASEE model. The Repertory Grid Interview used by Thunedborg *et al.* (1993) was compared with the General Health Questionnaire and the HAMA in a short-term study with patients suffering from General Anxiety Disorder. The results of this study showed, first, that it was meaningful for the interviewer to help the patient design his or her own grid of QOL within the PCASEE model (Table I). Second, it was found possible to estimate the percentage of improvement on the individual grid dimensions. Third, this Repertory Grid Interview was found to be more sensitive than the General Health Questionnaire or the HAMA to measure treatment outcome (Thunedborg *et al.*, 1993).

Another scale based on Kelly's Repertory Grid approach has been constructed by van Dam *et al.* (1991). A key issue in the application of any rating scale is 'the measure of change' (Cronbach and Furby, 1970).

In the case of idiographic and disease-specific QOL scales, the index of change often used in long-term trials in patients with chronic disorders is percentage improvement, expressed as the gain in post-treatment score as a percentage of the distance between the pre-treatment score and the patient's own ideal goal for treatment. As discussed elsewhere (Bech, 1990), the concept of improvement refers to a clinical distance along which the current state of the patient's post-treatment score is compared with the pre-treatment position on the one hand, and the intended goal of treatment on the other. The Repertory Grid Interview (Thunedborg *et al.*, 1993) gives this global index of improvement which is based on a multivariate analysis of PCASEE dimensions. Thereby QOL measurement is considered as an extra outcome criterion of the treatment under study.

However, no standard criteria for clinical change have been determined in long-term treatment. Among such criteria Sullivan (1992) has suggested the following: (a) the overall judgement of improvement or deterioration by a patient and his or her physician; (b) an agreed way of combining the patient's and a physician's independent assessment; and (c) a significant change in specific variables over time.

From a statistical point of view, however, this multiple endpoint approach can give problems. The various statistical methods to adjust for multiple outcome scores in clinical trials using QOL data have been discussed by Tandon (1990).

SBQOL: a nomothetic scale with idiographic features

This section will focus on the development and characteristics of the SmithKline Beecham QOL Scale (SBQOL), a nomothetic scale which incorporates, as an integral element of its design, features typical of the idiographic approach.

Assuming that QOL is an internal or subjective experience, if it is to be measured, it must be defined in some way. Generally, a person's perception of their own QOL is the result of input from three areas of functioning: mental, physical and social. Any scale purporting to measure QOL must contain relevant items tapping each of these areas. Since QOL is a subjective experience, any measure must also be able to reflect this egocentricity. The most direct way of making such an assessment is by asking the subject or patient to rate themselves. Consider someone with reduced sleep. An observer can objectively record sleep reduced from say 7 or 5 hours. However, it is the person's experience of the reduced quality of sleep that is most important. This subjectivity is at the very centre of QOL measurement. Recently, the WHO endorsed this fundamental approach to QOL measurement (WHO, 1991), stating 'the individual himself/herself should be the arbiter of their quality of life'.

If subjectivity is at the heart of QOL assessment, against what can it be measured in order to obtain some idea of impairment? Calman (1984) has suggested that QOL is 'the difference at a particular period of time, between the hopes and expectations of the individual and the individual's present experience'. An abstraction of 'ideal self' could thus be used to assess QOL at any given moment in time. Any change in the difference between 'self now' and 'ideal self' could then be used as a measure in change of QOL.

Components of SBQOL
From the foregoing discussion it is clear there is a need for a scale which can measure this egocentric concept of QOL. Further, the essential components of a new scale, the SBQOL, can be derived. Thus the scale should:

1.   Have items relating to the main areas of experience relevant to QOL.
2.   Be a self-rating scale.
3.   Be structured in such a way that the subject assesses their present QOL against a personalized ideal standard.

Each of these aspects of SBQOL will be considered further.

Items of SBQOL
Consideration of literature sources indicates that a relatively limited number of areas of experience are subsumed under the rubric of mental, physical and social well-being. In the development of SBQOL, 10 such domains were considered. These are listed in Table II.

Table II.   Domains selected to be important in assessing QOL.

Sense of psychic well-being
Physical well-being (especially pain and mobility)
Social relationships
Activities/hobbies/interests
Mood
Locus of control
Sexual function
Work/employment
Religion
Finances

Within these domains more specific areas of experience were identified, these being called 'constructs', following nomenclature used with repertory grid techniques (Kelly, 1955; Beal, 1985). In the early evolution of SBQOL, repertory grid technique greatly influenced the development process. The very great attraction of this technique was that a subject used 'elements' which are the object of their thoughts, e.g. father, and constructs which were the qualities they used to think about the elements, e.g. loving. Repertory grid allows a highly egocentric picture to be generated of that person's way of viewing the outside world. This great subjectivity was required in SBQOL. The elements selected were 'self now', 'ideal self' and 'sick self' since these were felt to be appropriate for people assessing their life quality in the setting of therapy for a disease process. The present list of constructs used in SBQOL are given in Table III.

Self-rating scale

So that the subjective nature of QOL could be assessed directly a self-rating technique was employed. Initially a pencil-and-paper test was used. However, to increase user friendliness and to reduce the input needed from an invigilator, a computerized system was developed. In this way the attractor of SBQOL was increased for both the respondent and the user.

Table III.   Construct categories of SBQOL by domain.

Psychic well-being	*Social relationships*
Cope with problems	Make friends/relationships
Feel secure	Feel wanted
Comfortable with self	Feel inferior
Feel a failure	
Feel confident	*Work/employment*
Feel useful	Satisfaction with work
	Cope at work
Physical well-being	
Sleep	*Activities/interests/hobbies*
Physical mobility	Pleasure from leisure time
Energy	
Pain	*Finance*
Appetite	Worried over money
Mood	*Sexual function*
Irritable	Satisfied with sex life
Worried	
Enjoy life	*Religion*
Without hope	Supported by faith
	Faith in religion
Locus of control	
Feel in control	
Decision-making	
Helplessness	

Structure

Initially SBQOL contained three elements, but during development this was reduced to two (see next section). The scale contains 28 constructs. Initially, the patient is asked to think about themselves as they are now. With this self-now mental set, they rate themselves on the 28 constructs, which are presented as a digitalized visual analogue scale (VAS). At each pole of the VAS the extremes of that construct are given, e.g. I sleep badly—I sleep very well. They are then asked to think of an ideal state, i.e. a personalized concept of perfect QOL—ideal self. With this ideal self mental set they then complete the 28 constructs a second time. When the SBQOL scale has been completed the data can be entered into the Flexigrid (Tschudi, 1990) computer program. This gives for each construct the distance between self now and ideal self in multidimensional space. It can also produce an inter-element distance for all constructs combined. Alternatively, more simple Euclidean distances can be calculated. The relative merits of each type of measurement are explored below.

Development of SBQOL

Initially, ten domains were selected which were thought to be important in measuring QOL (see Table II). These domains were taken from a literature review of scales used previously. Good agreement can be seen with the results of McGee *et al.* (1991), who elicited important QOL domains from a sample of normal subjects and patients attending a gastroenterology clinic. The major differences with SBQOL involved the areas of education and living conditions, which are not felt relevant to the internalized concept of QOL underpinning the present work. Using these 10 domains, a total of 74 items or constructs were generated, describing in more detail features of the domains.

An initial study (Study 1) was undertaken to reduce the number of constructs from 74 to more user-friendly proportions. A general population sample was recruited at centres in Liverpool, Newark, London and Hove. Following a face-to-face enrolment, subjects completed the first version (74 items) of the SBQOL. Over 1000 subjects were recruited and the results subjected to factor and cluster analysis. As a result, the number of constructs was reduced to 28 (Dunbar *et al.*, 1992). The final constructs are given in Table III.

As can be seen, not all domains contributed an equal number of constructs to the reduced questionnaire. Most items were selected from domains other than physical well-being. The relatively low status of physical health in QOL assessment is important since it has conceptual implications. Thus, although poor physical health will impact on QOL, it would be a mistake to concentrate on this measure alone. Because of this, the HRQOL scales may not be optimal in assessing QOL and in particular may not be sensitive to change.

It can be argued that this finding was a reflection of the population studied, i.e. well people. However, these results are in full accord with those of McGee *et al.* (1991). The latter found that physical health was often not an important

Table IV. Relative importance of SBQOL domains in a sample of psychiatric patients.

Domain	Ranking
Psychic well-being	2.4
Physical well-being	3.5
Mood	4.2
Locus of control	4.6
Social relationships	4.7
Work/employment	5.5
Activities/interests/hobbies	5.5
Finance	6.6
Sexual function	7.4
Religion	7.6

factor in QOL. Rather, family, social and leisure activities as well as psychological health were more important. To further assess this a study was undertaken in 20 psychiatric patients (Study 2) suffering from moderate–severe anxiety or depression (Dunbar and Stoker, 1992), according to DSM-III-R classification (1987). They were given the 10 domains selected to measure QOL and asked to rank them in order of importance for their own QOL. The results are given in Table IV. These results further support the importance of psychological well-being in assessing QOL for this group of patients. In the same study no spontaneously generated domains were identified which were not already included in SBQOL.

A validation and reliability study of the SBQOL has also been undertaken (Stoker *et al.*, 1992). In this trial 129 patients seen in general practice with mild to moderate anxiety or depression according to DSM-III-R (American Psychiatric Association, 1987) were assessed. Patients were treated at the discretion of their general practitioner (GP) and followed up over a period of 12 weeks. Efficacy was assessed and the SBQOL administered at baseline, week 6 and week 12. In this study, 23 and not 28 constructs were used, since a number of the minor constructs, including those on sex and religion, had been found inappropriate to 15% of the sample from Study 1. The Hamilton Depression Rating Scale (HAM-D) or Anxiety Scale (HAMA) were used as efficacy variables. Construct validity was assessed by examining the relationship between changes in the SBQOL scale scores during the course of treatment and the corresponding change in symptomatic status as assessed by the HAM-D or HAMA.

Concurrent validity was assessed using the Sickness Impact Profile (SIP) (Bergner *et al.*, 1981), as an external criterion. Correlations between the SIP and the HAM-D or HAMA were calculated, as was the correlation between SBQOL and a negative control, i.e. a scale measuring variables with which a QOL scale would not be expected to be related. In this study the Eysenck personality questionnaire (EPQ) (Eysenck, 1976) was used to provide the negative control measures. The test–retest reliability was also measured with patients completing the SBQOL on the day before therapy started and one day later.

Results for construct validity are given in Figures 1 and 2. Both the self now/ sick self and self now/ideal self distances are given over time, as are both the Euclidean and Flexigrid distances. A high positive correlation was found between the self now/ideal self distance and the HAM-D or HAMA. A high negative correlation was found between the self now/sick self distance and these same efficacy variables. These results provided good evidence of construct validity for the SBQOL scale.

Results for concurrent validity are given in Figure 3, which shows the relationship between the SIP total score and the SBQOL inter-element distance measures during treatment. Change in SIP score over time for all patients is plotted against SBQOL distances. A high correlation was again found between the external criterion and the SBQOL distances, this being positive for the self now/ideal self and negative for the self now/sick self distances. A much lower correlation was found between SBQOL distances and the 'E' (extroversion) scale of the EPQ. The good correlation between the SIP and the poor correlation with the EPQ 'E' scale provided strong evidence of concurrent validity for the SBQOL scale.

Inspection of both Figures 1 and 2 showed that the self now/ideal self and self now/sick self plots were almost mirror images of one another. This suggested a degree of redundancy in the data and, as a result, in further development work only the self now/ideal self distance was assessed. A further important result of this study can be seen in Figures 1–3 by comparing the two SBQOL distances. Both the simple Euclidean and the more complex computer-generated Flexigrid distances correlated equally will with the external criterion. The Flexigrid distances were correlated slightly more highly, but the increase in association did not seem to justify the much more complex method of distance calculation. As a result it was decided to dispense with the use of the Flexigrid programme and instead simply calculate Euclidean distances.

The results of this important study can be summarized as follows:

1. Good reliability and validity data were generated, which included construct and concurrent validity and test–retest and split half reliability.
2. Major changes in the format of SBQOL were implemented such that only the self now/ideal self distance was used and Euclidean distances rather than Flexigrid distances calculated.

A further study was undertaken to assess the degree of consistency of results between the pencil-and-paper version of SBQOL and the electronic (computerized) interface. Results are given in Table V. A high correlation was found indicating that investigators could use either the pencil-and-paper version or the computerized version since the results were almost interchangeable.

122

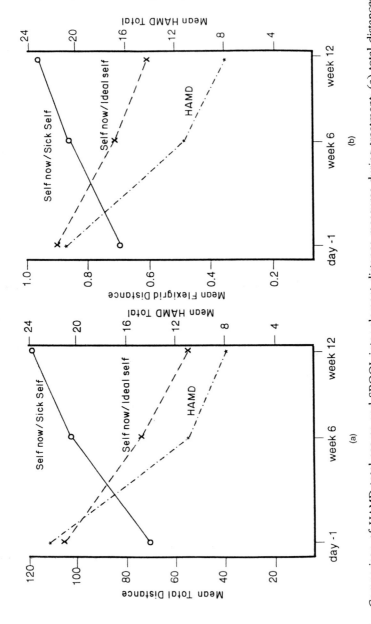

Figure 1. Comparison of HAMD total scores and SBQOL inter-element distance measures during treatment: (a) total distances; (b) Felxigrid distances.

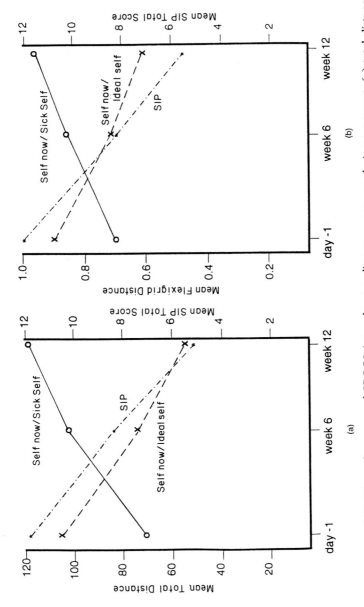

Figure 2. Comparison of HAMA total scores and SBQOL inter-element distance measures during treatment: (a) total distances; (b) Flexigrid distances.

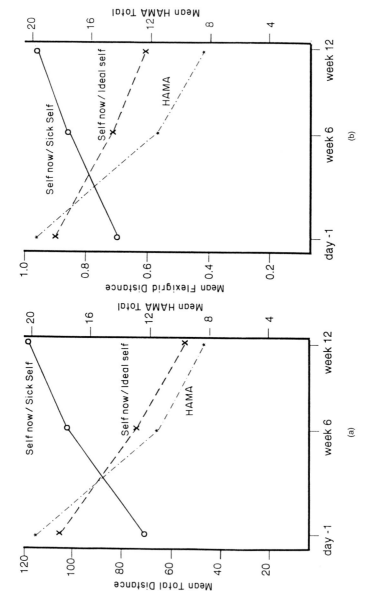

Figure 3. Comparison of SIP total scores and SBQOL inter-element distance measures during treatment: (a) total distances; (b) Flexigrid distances.

Table V. Correlation coefficients for inter-element distances between pencil-and-paper and computerized versions of SBQOL.

Paper	Electronic	
	Self now/ideal self	Self now/sick self
Self now/ideal self	0.93	—
Self now/sick self	—	0.78

In Study 3, described earlier, an apparent redundancy was noted, since the change in self now/ideal self and self now/sick self distances seemed to be mirror images of one another. Further, correlations with the external criterion were higher for self now/ideal self, indicating the potential redundancy of the self now/ sick self distance measure. To check whether this was correct, a further study (Dunbar and Stoker, 1992) was undertaken (Study 5) using the computerized form of SBQOL. Twenty anxious or depressed patients were recruited and given the two-element version and the three-element version in random order. Patients were aged 18–75 years, were male or female and completed each version within a 24-hour time period. The impact of either collecting or not collecting self now/ sick self data on self now/ideal self data can be seen in Table VI. No difference was found, indicating that if self now/ideal self distance was of most interest, then this could be assessed with or without assessment of the sick self. These results further support the notion that the self now/ideal self distance will be adequate alone, as a sensitive measure of change in QOL.

Further plans
Some of the complexities of developing a QOL scale have been reviewed with reference to the new SBQOL scale. Presently a scale exists which has some substance, but is as yet far from being a fully developed scale. Further plans involve additional validation and reliability studies. In particular, a multicentre study has been initiated which will assess the usefulness of SBQOL in a variety of clinical settings, including general practice and psychiatric outpatient clinics. A wide variety of different types of patient will be enrolled and the study will afford the possibility of assessing SBQOL in European languages other than English. A further refinement has been introduced in which, after completing

Table VI. The effect of collecting or not collecting self now/sick self data on self now/ ideal self inter-element distance.

	Two-element version	Three-element version
Self now/ideal self distance	510	554

Pearson's correlation coefficient $r = 0.94$.
Paired t-test, $p = 0.22$.

the scale, the patient gives a weighting for each construct in terms of its importance in their personal evaluation of QOL. By weighting the constructs in this
way the egocentricity of the scale is further enhanced. This study will also
enable further reduction in the number of constructs if found appropriate.
Finally, a questionnaire based on the SBQOL experiences has been developed
covering the PCASEE model (Bech, 1993).

Conclusions

The US Food and Drug Administration (FDA) has set up several psychometric
requirements for a QOL scale (Shoemaker *et al.*, 1990), among them that the
scale should measure a dimension different from the 'raw' health data (clinical
disability), but also different from adverse drug reactions. QOL should not only
be considered of importance from a regulatory perspective, in applications for
new drugs (Westman-Naeser, 1992), but also in the post-marketing area; QOL
measures provide the most useful information for drugs, such as antidepressants, aimed at long-term or prophylactic treatment.

The SBQOL is considered to fulfil the psychometric properties specified by
the FDA for a scale purporting to measure QOL. The scale assumes QOL is an
internal concept, and assessment of QOL is made against a personalized concept of ideal self. Changes in QOL are measured by changes in the self now/
ideal self inter-element distance. At present the scale consists of constructs
describing the domains felt to be of major importance for QOL.

These features of the scale, taken together with data regarding the extent of
the association between changes in the QOL measure and changes in measures
of clinical disability, indicate that the SBQOL is measuring a dimension different
from 'raw' health measures and adverse drug reactions.

Finally, clinical studies in psychiatric patients indicate that the scale has construct and concurrent validity as well as good test–retest and internal consistency reliability.

References

American Psychiatric Association (1980) *Diagnostic and Statistical Manual of Mental
Disorders*, 3rd edn (DSM-III). Washington, DC: APA.
American Psychiatric Association (1987) *Diagnostic and Statistical Manual of Mental
Disorders*, 3rd edn—revised (DSM-III-R). Washington, DC: APA.
Angst G, Stassen HH and Delini-Stula A (1992) Onset of improvement under antidepres-
sant treatment: a survival analytic approach. Paper presented at the Strasbourg
Forum, 18–19 June 1992.
Beal N (1985) *Repertory Grid Technique and Personal Constructs: Application in Clini-
cal and Educational Settings*. Beckenham: Croom Helm.

Bech P (1987) Quality of life in psychosomatic research. *Psychopathology* **20**, 169–179.

Bech P (1989) Clinical effects of selective serotonin reuptake inhibitors. In: Dahl SG and Gram LF (eds) *Clinical Pharmacology in Psychiatry*. Berlin: Springer.

Bech P (1990) Measurements of psychological distress and well-being. *Psychother Psychosom* **54**, 77–89.

Bech P (1992) *Rating Scales for Psychopathology, Health Status, and Quality of Life: A Compendium on Documentation in Accordance with the DSM III R and WHO Systems*. Berlin: Springer.

Bech P and Coppen A (1990) *The Hamilton Scales*. Berlin: Springer.

Bergner M, Bobbit RA, Carter W and Gilson B (1981) The sickness impact profile: development and final revision of a health status measure. *Med Care* **19**, 787–805.

Calman KC (1984) Quality of life in cancer patients: an hypothesis. *J Med Ethics* **10**, 124–127.

Chrischilles EA (1992) The contribution of epidemiology to pharmacoeconomic research. *Drug Information J* **26**, 219–229.

Cronbach LJ and Furby L (1970) How we should measure change—or should we? *Psychol Bull* **74**, 68–80.

Croog SH, Levin S and Testa M (1986) The effects of antihypertensive therapy on the quality of life. N Engl *J Med* **314**, 1657–1667.

Dunbar GC and Stoker MJ (1992) The development of a questionnaire to measure quality of life in psychiatric patients. *Br J Med Econ* **4**, 63–73.

Dunbar GC, Stoker MJ, Hodges TCP and Beaumont G (1992) The development of SBQOL: a unique scale for measuring the quality of life. *Br J Med Econ* **2**, 65–74.

Dupuy HJ (1984) The psychological general well-being (PGWB) index: an assessment of quality of life in clinical trials of cardiovascular therapies. In: Wenger NK, Mattson ME, Furberg CD and Elison J (eds) New York: Le Jacq, pp 184–188.

Edwards BC, Lambert MJ, Moran PW *et al.* (1984) A meta-analytic comparison of the Beck Depression Inventory and the Hamilton Rating Scale for Depression as measures of treatment outcome. *Br J Clin Psychol* **23**, 93–99.

Eysenck HJ (1976) *The Measurement of Personality*. Baltimore: Park Press.

Eysenck HJ (1991) *Rebel with a Cause: An Autobiography*. London: WH Allen.

Feighner JP and Boyer WF (1991) *Selective Serotonin Reuptake Inhibitors*. Chichester: Wiley.

Goldberg D (1972) *The Detection of Psychiatric Illness by Questionnaires*. Oxford: Oxford University Press.

Guy W (1976) *Early Clinical Drug Evaluation (ECDEU) Assessment Manual for Psychopharmacology*. Rockville: National Institute of Mental Health.

Hamilton M (1967) Development of a rating scale for primary depressive illness. *Br J Soc Clin Psychol* **6**, 278–296.

Hamilton M (1977) Standard criteria for clinical assessment in psychopathology. *Drugs Exp Clin Res* **1**, 101–105.

Hunt SM and McKenna SP (1992) A British adaptation of the General Well-being Index: a new tool for clinical research. *Br J Med Econ* **2**, 49–60.

Joyce CRB (1992) Need for new models and methods assessing health-related quality of life. *Int J Methods Psychiatr Res* (in press).

Kelly GA (1955) *The Psychology of Personal Constructs*. New York: Norton.

Kinney JM and Stephens MAP (1989) Caregiving Hassles Scale: assessing the daily hassles of caring for a family member with dementia. *Gerontologist* **29**, 328–332.

McGee HM, O'Boyle CA, Hickey A, O'Malley K and Joyce CRB (1991) Assessing the quality of life of the individual: the SEIQoL with a healthy and gastroenterology unit population. *Psychol Med* **21**, 749–759.

Montgomery SA and Rouillon F (1992) *Long-term Treatment of Depression.* Chichester: Wiley.

Shoemaker D, Burke G, Door A, Temple R and Friedman MA (1990) A regulatory perspective. In: Spilker R (ed.) *Quality of Life in Clinical Trials.* New York: Raven Press, pp 193–201.

Stoker MJ, Dunbar GC and Beaumont G (1992) The SBQOL quality of life scale: a validation and reliability study in patients with affective disorder. *Quality Life Res* **1**, 385–395.

Sullivan M (1992) Quality of life assessment in medicine: concepts, definition and basic tools. *Nordic J Psychiatry* **46**, 79–84.

Tandon PK (1990) Application of global statistics in analysing quality of life data. *Stat Med* **9**, 819–827.

Thunedborg K, Allerup P, Bech P and Joyce CRB (1993) Development of the repertory grid for measurement of individual quality of life in clinical trials. *International Journal of Methods in Psychiatric Research* **3**, 45–56.

Tynman-Qua HG, De Jonghe F, McKenna S and Hunt S (1992) Quality of life in depression scale. Houtem: Ibero Publications.

Tschudi F (1990) Flexigrid, v 5.1 copyright 1990. University of Oslo, Norway.

van Dam FSAM, Somer R and van Bee-Cosijn AL (1991) Quality of life: some theoretical issues. *J Clin Pharmacol* **21**, 1665–1685.

Walker SR and Asscher W (1987) *Medicines and Risk/Benefit Decisions.* Lancaster: MTP Press.

Westman-Naeser S (1992) Regulatory aspects on quality of life measurements. *Nordic J Psychiatry* **46**, 101–104.

World Health Organization (1980) *International Classification of Impairments, Disabilities and Handicaps* (ICIDH). Geneva: WHO.

World Health Organization (1991) Meeting on the assessment of quality of life in health care, Geneva, 11–15 February 1991, MNH/PSF/914.

9

Social aspects of treating depression

D.J. Currie, D.B. Fairweather and I. Hindmarch

Introduction

Depression can be defined as a persistent feeling that the self is worthless, the world meaningless and the future hopeless. Feeling miserable and sad is a common experience to most of us; however, there is a significant difference between this and those symptoms which characterize clinical depression, albeit a continuum seems to exist between normal human sadness through neurotic misery to psychotic delusions.

Many sufferers of depression fear being considered as malingerers and have feelings of guilt for their condition. In Western society particularly, the widely held ethic of being firm and standing on one's own feet is likely to augment these feelings of guilt and unworthiness among depressed individuals to the extent that suicide may seem the only way out. The disparagement and mistrust with which depressive illness continues to be regarded by both sufferers and onlookers alike helps to explain why depression remains under-reported, under-diagnosed and under-treated.

While it is true that there exists a greater degree of sympathy and understanding towards the sufferers of depression than there was in the past, and with an increasing realization that it is a serious illness rather than a trivial condition from which one can simply 'pull oneself together', it is estimated that only 25% of cases of depression are actually recognized and treated (West, 1992). This brings us on to the so-called iceberg of depression, with only the tip visible as clinically diagnosed depression (Figure 1). Many depression sufferers do not

---

Health Economics of Depression. Edited by B. Jönsson and J. Rosenbaum

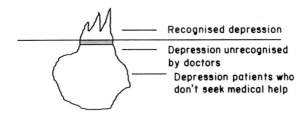

Figure 1.   The iceberg of depression (From Kelly, D. (1987)).

seek medical care and it is claimed that general practitioners (GPs) miss as many cases as they diagnose (Tylee, 1991). Patients with unrecognized depression have been regarded as being less severely depressed as those who seek treatment, but others believe that there is little or no difference in severity between the two groups.

Treatment

There appears to be no definitive biological markers of depression and thus clinicians rely on the patients' symptoms to assess the need for intervention. Severe manifestations of depression such as melancholia or delusionary states indicate the use of medicines or electroconvulsant therapy (ECT) and, in some cases, drug therapy may be augmented by psychotherapy.

Depressive states are believed to have a chemical basis characterized by imbalances in the monoamine and serotoninergic systems in the brain. The rationale for medical intervention is to use antidepressant drugs aimed at correcting these abnormalities, and it has been estimated that 60–65% of depressed patients show a definite improvement with pharmacological treatment (Sacco and Beck, 1985).

Monoamine oxidase inhibitors
The first drugs to be introduced clinically as antidepressants were the monoamine oxidase inhibitors (MAOIs) (Crane, 1957), and while these older, hydrazine-derived MAOIs have proved to be valuable in the treatment of depression and other psychiatric disorders, the adverse effects associated with them remain, such as potentiation of the pressor effect of tyramine found in certain foodstuffs. These early MAO inhibitors have since been largely superseded by the tricyclic antidepressants (TCAs).

Tricyclic antidepressants
There are several tricyclic antidepressants (TCAs) available on the UK market, including imipramine (the parent compound), amitriptyline, dothiepin,

desipramine and doxepin. However, the high toxicity and high incidence of long-term treatment side effects which often accompany TCA therapy have limited their usage in many depressed patients. As these drugs are broadly equipotent in their antidepressant efficacy, the choice of which to use should be governed by the unwanted side effects, for example, orthostatic hypotension or sedation (Potter *et al.*, 1991).

All the TCAs produce the classical anticholinergic side effects, including dry mouth, constipation, urinary retention, blurred vision and confusion—effects which the elderly find particularly difficult to tolerate. Some TCAs, however, are more sedating (particularly amitriptyline), whereas others are usually more activating (desipramine).

Dissatisfaction with these antidepressants has directed research towards new therapeutics which are safer and therefore more effective in improving clinical outcome.

Reversible inhibitors of MAO type A

A new generation of MAOIs known as the reversible inhibitors of MAO type A (RIMAs) are becoming available and have been launched in several markets. They appear to be less sensitive to the tyramine reaction and there are claims that they are relatively free from both anticholinergic and sedative effects. It is still too early, however, to fully assess the true value of these new drugs and their place in the clinical management of depression.

Selective serotonin reuptake inhibitors

Increased appreciation of the role of serotonin in depression has led to the development of highly selective inhibitors of serotonin reuptake which have little influence on noradrenaline or dopamine systems—characteristics which distinguish them from conventional TCAs. Consequently, these selective serotonin reuptake inhibitors (SSRIs) provide effective antidepressant activity without the sedating, anticholinergic or cardiotoxic reactions seen with the older antidepressant drugs.

The major advantage of SSRIs is that they are apparently very well tolerated and have a low lethality in overdose (Schatzberg and Cole, 1986), thereby significantly reducing the suicide risk. The advantages of SSRIs have seen fluoxetine replace the TCAs in the USA between 1987 and 1990 as the leading choice of antidepressant for most types of depression. This group of compounds are non-sedating, which represents a significant benefit over the sedating TCAs in the context of the risk of accidents, daytime functioning and overall quality of life, which are issues expanded on later in this chapter. There are four SSRIs currently available in the UK and clinical trials have shown them to be clinically equipotent to the TCAs in alleviating depression.

Consequences of antidepressant therapy

Overdose and suicide

The metabolism of the TCAs varies greatly (Rudorfer and Potter, 1989); therefore it of utmost importance that doses are carefully tailored to each individual patient. The TCAs have a narrow therapeutic window where, in addition to the risk of plasma levels falling to sub-therapeutic levels, there is the much greater danger of toxicity through overdose. Overdose with TCAs is likely to be lethal and depressed patients with suicidal tendencies are particularly at risk and so should be prescribed TCAs with great caution in limited quantities. As little as five to six times the maximal daily dose of imipramine can prove fatal (Potter *et al.*, 1991).

The SSRIs have a clear advantage over alternative antidepressants in this respect, since to date no fatalities with overdosage of SSRIs have been reported. A patient survived after ingesting 8600 mg of fluvoxamine, which is nearly 30 times the recommended daily dose. Furthermore, a total of 19 patients have taken overdoses of paroxetine in amounts of up to 1000 mg, either alone or in combination with another agent, and in each case there has been a full recovery.

The majority of those suffering from depression do not attempt suicide and, of those who do try, most do not succeed. However, about 70% of suicide victims are considered to be suffering from depression and about 15% of depressives eventually commit suicide (Wilkinson, 1989). There are an estimated 100 000 cases of deliberate self-harm every year.

Using national mortality statistics and prescription data for England, Wales and Scotland, Cassidy and Henry have compiled fatal toxicity indices for the commonly available antidepressants (Table I). These data demonstrate that three of the earlier TCAs (desipramine, dothiepin and amitriptyline) have a higher fatality index than the mean of all antidepressants, and that imipramine, trazodone and mianserin have a lower index, suggesting that the latter may be safer. Table II shows data on suicides linked to overdose with antidepressants collected in Ireland over 17-year period from 1971 to 1988 (Kelleher *et al.*, 1992). A similar pattern emerges, with the older tricyclic compounds scoring alarmingly high.

Table I. Fatal poisonings 1975–1984 for antidepressant drugs in England, Wales and Scotland.

Drug	Deaths per million prescriptions (95% confidence intervals)
Desipramine	80.2**
Dothiepin	50.0***
Amitriptyline	46.5***
Imipramine	28.4***
Trazodone	13.6*
Mianserin	5.6***
All antidepressants	34.9

Significant differences compared to all antidepressants, * $p < 0.05$, ** $p < 0.01$, *** $p < 0.001$. Adpated from Cassidy and Henry (1987).

Table II. Total number of suicides due to drug overdose in Ireland, 1971–1988.

Drug	No.
Amitriptyline	65
Imipramine	17
Dothiepin	16
Trazodone	1
Zimeldine	1
Mianserin	1

Adapted from Kelleher *et al.* (1992).

When a depressed patient attempts suicide by overdosing, the acute toxicity or safety of a drug is often the deciding factor regarding the outcome (de Jonghe and Swinkels, 1992). An outpatient prescription, which is usually at least a two-week supply, can provide the patient with a sufficient amount for a life-threatening overdose. According to de Jonghe and Swinkels (1992), an anti-depressant is 'safe' if 14 times the therapeutic daily dose (TD) does not exceed the lethal dose (LD). For example, amitriptyline and dothiepin are considered to have an antidepressant action at a TD of 150–300 mg and the LD is estimated at 2500 mg. As ingestion of 14 days' supply of these drugs exceeds the LD, they are regarded as 'less safe' in overdose. Other drugs such as the SSRIs paroxetine and fluoxetine have a TD of 20 mg and are therefore considered 'safe' as far as acute toxicity is concerned.

Behavioural toxicity
Drugs which affect psychomotor performance and cognitive function can be said to possess behavioural toxicity. The measurement of this toxicity is an important task of the psychopharmacologist; the importance stems from the following three reasons. First, changes in psychomotor function represent one of the truly objective assessments of the psychoactive property of a drug. Second, because psychological test batteries are often analogues of the essential aspects of real life behaviour, changes in these tests go some way to predict the impact that a drug would have on a real task such as driving a car. Third, since it has been proposed that both mental and psychomotor retardation are a primary expression of depressive illness (Widlocher 1983a,b), psychomotor and cognitive tests can be used to measure the extent to which a putative antidepressant affects these psychological functions. Furthermore, the severity of depression has been linked to the extent of psychomotor retardation, in particular the inability to maintain motivation and attention (Cohen *et al.*, 1982).

Psychopharmacological testing can thus indicate the 'safety' of a drug by establishing an index of its behavioural toxicity. It can also objectively determine the magnitude of the drug's psychoactive properties, and the extent to which a particular compound affects information-processing and cognitive function. Substances which have a negative action on these aspects of psychological integrity can be regarded as counter-therapeutic because they make both psychomotor and mental functions worse, thus hindering improvement in some of the psychic manifestations of depression (Hindmarch 1987, 1988). Drugs which increase arousal can also be behaviourally toxic and thereby disrupt therapy and lifestyle. As one might expect, the optimum aim for therapeutic agents is to achieve psychomotor neutrality or zero behavioural toxicity.

For the antidepressants in particular, psychometric measure which focus on aspects of information-processing and psychomotor function have been shown to be relatively sensitive indicators of their cognitive and therapeutic effects in patients (Birren *et al.*, 1980; Siegfried, 1989; Widlocher and Ghozlan, 1989). A number of antidepressants of the tricyclic type, notably amitriptyline, imipramine and desipramine, have consistently been reported as producing sedative effects (Hanks, 1984; Hindmarch and Parrott, 1977; Hindmarch, 1988), as have some non-tricyclic compounds, e.g. the atypical antidepressant trazodone and the tetracyclic mianserin (Hindmarch and Subhan, 1986).

The newer classes of antidepressants, such as the SSRIs, appear to lack the profoundly sedating properties of the older agents. Examples are: paroxetine (Hindmarch and Harrison, 1988b); fluoxetine (Hindmarch, 1987; Hindmarch and Harrison, 1988a); zimeldine (Hindmarch *et al.*, 1983); fluvoxamine (Hindmarch *et al.*, 1990); sertraline (Hindmarch and Bhatti, 1988); and cericlamine (Hindmarch *et al.*, 1990). Moclobemide, a novel MAOI-A inhibitor, also appears to be free from any notable behavioural side effects (Hindmarch and Kerr, 1991).

The tests which have been used to determine the performance effects of antidepressants include the critical flicker fusion threshold (CFF) and the choice reaction time test (CRT). The CFF provides an indication of the state of arousal of the central nervous system by measuring the capacity to process information, and the CRT gives a measure of sensorimotor performance which may be regarded as an analogue of the ability to carry out everyday activities. In addition to these basic tests, the effects of antidepressants on specific tasks of psychomotor coordination and other cognitive processes have been investigated.

Effects on memory function

The impact of different antidepressants on the variables of memory function has recently been reviewed by Thompson (1991), where he highlighted a number of difficulties with many of the studies carried out in this area. The suggestion was made that the majority fail to sufficiently take into account that depression itself can adversely affect memory; therefore changes in memory performance are confounded by alleviation of the depressive symptoms. He also points out the large variability in both dosage and duration of treatment and that the time at which memory assessment is carried out may be a possible source of misleading data because of the differences in pharmacokinetics between antidepressants. This was cited by Curran *et al.* (1988) as the reason why they failed to detect any effect of protriptyline on memory function. They noted that this drug takes 8–12 hours to reach peak plasma concentration, in comparison to the other three drugs in their study, which took between 2 and 4 hours. The final problem highlighted as the one which continues to beset all psychometric research, that being the diverse nature of the testing procedures which have been used. This makes the comparison across studies difficult, particularly as different tests measure different aspects of memory function.

Despite these caveats, the available evidence suggests that antidepressant drugs can exert an impact on memory, both directly and indirectly. Detrimental effects on a range of memory functions have been reported with amitriptyline, mianserin and trazodone (Curran *et al.*, 1988). The newer SSRI compounds, namely zimeldine, fluvoxamine and fluoxetine, have been shown to have a neutral effect on memory (Linnoila *et al.*, 1983; Eckhart *et al.*, 1986; Moskovitz and Burns, 1988), and one report indicates that fluvoxamine may exert a beneficial influence on memory processes in memory-impaired individuals (Martin *et al.*, 1989).

Effects on sleep and anxiety

The newer drugs do not have the day-time sedative effects of the older antidepressants (see above), and there is evidence to suggest that the SSRIs improve sleep. Paroxetine, for example, has been shown to have a beneficial effect on sleep quality, as assessed by the Leeds Sleep Evaluation Questionnaire, when compared to dothiepin and mianserin (Dorman, 1990). In addition, it has been demonstrated that paroxetine reduced anxiety associated with depression, compared to baseline, with a similar efficacy to amitriptyline (Hutchison *et al.*, 1991).

Consequences of behavioural toxicity

Many of the antidepressants which are still widely prescribed, notably the tricyclics, have a generally high rating of behavioural toxicity. For these drugs it is important to urge caution with their use, especially for ambulant outpatients who may be involved in driving or operating machinery where impairment of psychomotor functions could place them at greater risk of accident. The concept of behaviourally toxic drugs is of particular relevance to the elderly, who may already be cognitively disadvantaged and more prone to accidents. In addition to the decreased patient safety and quality of life, those drugs that possess significant toxicity in this respect are counter-therapeutic in that they delay efficacious response to drug treatment. Furthermore, if the behavioural side effects are perceived by the patient, it may adversely affect drug compliance, thereby further mitigating against reliable therapy.

Accidents

When looking at the accidents associated with antidepressant use, it is clear that those TCAs with sedating properties significantly increase the risk of precipitating an accident in the home, at work or on the roads. Laboratory studies have shown that even low doses of amitriptyline slow brake reaction times by up to twice as much as four units of alcohol, which for many individuals raises the blood alcohol level above the legal limit for driving. It is an area of concern that in the UK the Civil Aviation Authority insist that airline pilots are grounded when they are on antidepressant therapy, whereas no analogous rules apply to train, bus or car drivers.

Epidemiological data indicate that in the elderly TCAs are associated with a 60% increase in the likelihood of sustaining a hip fracture through falls (Ray *et al.*, 1991). In another recent retrospective cohort study the same group monitored the risk of motor vehicle crashes and psychoactive drug use in a group of 16 262 elderly drivers over a five-year period. The results indicated that TCA use raised the relative risk by a factor of 2.2, with a 95% confidence interval ranging from 1.3 to 3.5. There was a pronounced trend of an increasing crash involvement risk with increasing dose. For TCAs, doses equal to or in excess of 125 mg (amitriptyline equivalent) were associated with a nearly six-fold increase in crash risk (Ray *et al.*, 1992). While these and other epidemiological studies (e.g. Granek *et al.*, 1987; Myers *et al.*, 1991) are not without their methodological and data interpretation difficulties, such findings remain a serious cause for concern, requiring closer investigation.

Cost of depression

TCAs have been available for over 30 years and have undoubtedly been effective in alleviating the suffering of depression, as well as reducing the demand on hospital beds and the use of electroconvulsive therapy (ECT). Today, response to the treatment of depression relies on a carefully considered balance between psychotherapy and pharmacological intervention. The advent of a new generation of antidepressants has widened the choice of treatment, but an important factor which must be take into consideration in acceptance of the newer drugs is their higher cost.

The SSRIs are significantly more expensive than the TCAs pill for pill. TCAs, however, are associated with poor tolerability and side effects which, by reducing compliance, increase the rate of relapses, thereby adding to the overall burden and costs on the health services. The value in terms of improved quality of life and reduced behavioural toxicity, with its implications for a reduction of accident risk, are other important factors indicating that SSRIs might be a better option in the long run: amitriptyline may be cheaper than an SSRI, but a single road traffic fatality costs around £800 000 on average (UK government figure).

Finally, all the signs are that SSRIs cannot be used as tools for suicide, and the value of this both in financial and human terms cannot be overstated. These factors must be weighed for their relative merit in considering the relative costs of treatment. These and other important economic aspects of the pharmacological treatment of depression are dealt with in an earlier chapter.

Conclusion

With respect to antidepressant drugs, the debate continues over whether TCAs should retain their dominant position as the drugs of choice, or give way to the newer drugs, as they are beginning to do in the USA. In the UK it remains to be seen whether the view of Livingstone (1990) will prevail, that TCAs will continue to have a major role to play, with the newer entities offering an alternative for special cases, or that of Johnson (1991), that the SSRIs represent a major advance in the reduction of toxicity, safety in overdose and patient tolerance.

References

Birren JE, Woods AM and Williams MV (1980) Behavioural slowing with age: causes, organisation and consequences. In: Pook LW (ed.) *Aging in the 1980s: Psychological Issues*. Washington DC: APA.

Cassidy S and Henry J (1987) Fatal toxicity of antidepressant drugs in overdose. *Br Med J* **295**, 1021–1024.

Cohen RM, Weingartner H, Smallberg SA *et al.* (1982) Effort and cognition in depression. *Arch Gen Psychiatry* **39**, 593.

Crane GE (1957) Iproniazid (Marsilid) phosphate, a therapeutic agent for mental disorders and debilitating disease. *Psychiatr Res Rep* **8**, 142–152.

Curran HV, Sakulsriprong M and Lader M (1988) Antidepressants and human memory: an investigation of four drugs with different sedative and anticholinergic profiles. *Psychopharmacology* **95**, 520–527.

de Jonghe F and Swinkels JA (1992) The safety of antidepressants. *Drugs* **43** (Suppl. 2), 40–47.

Dorman T (1990) A double blind comparison of paroxetine and mianserin on sleep in elderly depressed hospital patients. Presented at the 17th CINP Congress, Kyoto, SB Pharmaceuticals.

Eckhardt MJ, Stapleton JM, Rio D *et al.* (1986) Interactions of fluvoxamine and ethanol in healthy volunteers. 15th Collegium Internationale Neuro-psychopharmacologicum, pp. 55–57. San Juan, Puerto Rico.

Granek E, Baker SP, Abbey H *et al.* (1987) Medications and diagnosis in relation to falls in a long term care facility. *J Am Geriatr Soc* **35**, 503–511.

Hanks GW (1984) The effects of amitriptyline and nomifensine on critical flicker fusion threshold in an elderly patient population. In: Linford-Rees W and Priest RG (eds) *Nomifensine: A Pharmacological and Clinical Profile*, pp. 87–94. Royal Society of Medicine International Congress and Symposium Series, No. 70. Oxford: Oxford University Press.

Hindmarch I (1987) Three antidepressants (amitriptyline, dothiepin, fluoxetine), with and without alcohol, compared with placebo on tests of psychomotor ability related to car driving. *Hum Psycopharmacol* **2**, 177.

Hindmarch I (1988) Information processing, critical flicker fusion threshold and benzodiazepines: results and speculations. In: Hindmarch I and Ott H (eds) *Benzodiazepine Receptor Ligands, Memory and Information Processing*, pp. 78–89. Heidelberg: Springer-Verlag.

Hindmarch I and Bhatti JZ (1988) Psychopharmacological effects of sertraline in normal healthy volunteers. *Eur J Clin Pharmacol* **35**, 221–223.

Hindmarch I and Harrison C (1988a) Three antidepressants (amitriptyline, dothiepin, fluoxetine) with and without alcohol, compared with placebo on tests of psychomotor ability related to car driving. *Hum Psychopharmacol* **2**, 177–183.

Hindmarch I and Harrison C (1988b) The effects of paroxetine and other antidepressants in combination with alcohol, in psychomotor activity related to car driving. *Hum Psychopharmacol* **3**, 13–20.

Hindmarch I and Kerr J (1991) The behavioural toxicity of antidepressants with particular reference to moclobemide. *Psychopharmacology* **106**, S49–S55.

Hindmarch I and Parrott AC (1977) Repeated dose comparisons of nomifensine, imipramine and placebo on subjective assessments of sleep and objective measures of psychomotor performance. *Br J Clin Pharmacol.* **4**, 167S–173S.

Hindmarch I and Subhan Z (1986) The effects of antidepressants, taken in conjunction with ethanol, on information processing and psychomotor performance related to car driving ability. In: O'Hanlon JF and de Gier JJ (eds) *Drugs and Driving*, pp. 231–240. London: Taylor & Francis.

Hindmarch I, Subhan Z and Stoker MJ (1983) The effects of zimeldine and amitriptyline on car driving and psychomotor performance. *Acta Psychiatr Scand* **68**, (Suppl. 308), 141.

Hindmarch, I Baksi A, Shillingford C and Guillon Y (1990) Effects of JO 1017, a new 5HT reuptake inhibitor, on psychoperformance and cognitive function. Unpublished report, Robens Institute, University of Surrey.

Hutchison DR *et al* (1991) A double blind comparison of paroxetine and amitriptyline in elderly depressed community patients. *Br J Clin Res* **2**, 43–47.

Johnson D (1991) The 5HT reuptake inhibitors: what place in therapy? *Prescriber* November.

Kelleher MJ, Daly M and Kelleher MJA (1992) The influence of antidepressants in overdose on the increased suicide rate in Ireland between 1971 and 1988. *Br J Psychiatry* **161**, 625–628.

Kelly D (1987) First and second generation antidepressants. In: Kelly D and France R (eds) *A Practical Handbook for the Treatment of Depression*. New Jersey: Parthenon.

Linnoila M, Johnson J, Dubyoski T *et al.* (1983) Effects of amitriptyline, desipramine and zimeldine, alone and in combination with ethanol, on information processing and memory in healthy volunteers. *Acta Psychiatr Scand* **68** (Suppl. 308), 175–181.

Livingstone M (1990) Tricyclic and newer antidepressants. *Prescribers' J* **30**, 139–147.

Martin PR, Adinoff B, Eckhardt MJ *et al.* (1989) Effective pharmacotherapy of alcoholic amnesic disorder with fluvoxamine. *Arch Gen Psychiatry* **46**, 617–621.

Moskowitz H and Burns M (1988) The effects on performance of two antidepressants alone and in combination with diazepam. *Prog Neuropsychopharmacol Biol Psychiatry* **12**, 783–792.

Myers AH, Baker SP, Van Natta ML, Abbey H and Robinson EG (1991) Risk factors associated with falls and injuries among elderly institutionalized persons. *Am J Epidemiol* **133**, 1179–1190.

Potter WZ, Rudorfer MV and Manji H (1991) The pharmacologic treatment of depression. *N Engl J Med* **325**, 633–642.

Ray WA, Griffin MR and Malcolm E (1991) Cyclic antidepressants and the risk of hip fracture. *Arch Intern Med* **151**, 754–756.

Ray WA, Fought RL and Decker MD (1992) Psychoactive drugs and the risk of injurious motor vehicle crashes in elderly drivers. *Am J Epidemiol.*, **136**, 873–883.

Rudorfer MV and Potter WZ (1989) The new generation of antidepressants. In: Extein IL (ed.) *Treatment of Tricyclic-resistant Depression.* Washington DC: American Psychiatric Press.

Sacco WP and Beck AT (1985) Cognitive theory of depression. In: Beckham EE and Leber WR (eds) *Handbook of Depression: Treatment, Assessment and Research.* Homewood, IL: Dorsey Press.

Schatzberg AF and Cole JO (1986) Antidepressants. In: *Manual of Clinical Pharmacology,* pp. 3–65. Washington, DC: American Psychiatric Press.

Siegfried K (1989) Toward a clinical classification of antidepressant profiles. In: Hindmarch I and Stonier P (eds) *Human psychopharmacology: Vol. 2. Measures and Methods,* pp. 141–154. Chichester: Wiley.

Thompson PJ (1991) Antidepressants and memory: a review. *Hum Psychopharmacol* **6**, 79–90.

Tylee A (1991) Recognising depression. *Practitioner* **235**, 669–672.

West R (1992) *Depression.* Current health problems No. 105. Office of Health Economics, London.

Widlocher DJ (1983a) Psychomotor retardation: clinical, theoretical and psychometric aspects. In: Akiskal HS (ed.) *The Psychiatric Clinics of North America,* Vol. 6. Philadelphia: Saunders.

Widlocher DJ (1983b) Retardation: a basic emotional response? In: Davis J, Maas J (eds) *The Affective Disorders.* New York: American Psychiatric Press.

Widlocher DJ and Ghozlan A (1989) The measurement of retardation in depression. In: Hindmarch I and Stonier P (eds) *Human Psychopharmacology. Vol. 2. Measures and Methods,* pp. 1–22. Chichester: Wiley.

Wilkinson DG (1989) *Depression: Recognition and Treatment in General Practice.* Oxford: Radcliffe Medical Press.

10

Clinical choices, cost-effectiveness and antidepressant treatments

Jerrold F. Rosenbaum

The healthcare environment, particularly in the United States, is a changing one, and it is all about money. Many clinicians have come to appreciate that the sobriquet 'managed care' is, in practice, a euphemism for 'managed money' and restricted care. The clinical world which we will leave to our trainees will be a very different one from that which drew us to medicine. In the classic painting of 'The Doctor' by Sir Luke Fildes, the physician, contemplating an ill child, while limited in his therapeutic armamentarium, had no doubt that he would attempt to do all that was possible. And yet, the technology of all that was possible then was contained in a small black bag while the other critical resources were the physician's time, effort and clinical experience. However, with the development and use of expensive drugs and technology, often applied in a hospital setting, the values driving physicians behavior, we are told, must shift; the values driving physician behaviour, we are told, must shift; all that is possible must become all that is feasible within economic constraints, all that is cost-effective. As the US awaits the emergence of a new healthcare policy and as public financing of healthcare increases over time in all countries, the mission of therapeutics becomes integrated with the reality of economic constraints in the concept of 'cost-effectiveness.' *Choices* will have to be made. Choices mean fewer and not more options and that the 'greater good' will at times override the individual good. The reality of limitation of resources is unfortunately that a clinical good for an individual patient may determine adverse consequences for many others in society.

Health Economics of Depression. Edited by B. Jönsson and J. Rosenbaum
© 1993 John Wiley & Sons Ltd.

A highly publicized example in the United States involved a genetically engineered, breakthrough treatment for a congenital enzyme deficiency disease. The patient, a young boy from a poor Latin American country, was able to receive life-sustaining treatment for a period of six months by the biotech company that had engineered the agent, with the understanding that the country would eventually pick up the cost of the treatment and approve the treatment for use in that country when the child returned home. The treatment, if approved, would cost many tens of thousands of dollars a year, in a country where a public health nurse earned less than $100 per month.

Thus, with a limited pool of resources to pay for the care of all, an era of guidelines and constraints is upon us. Each patient is viewed as inextricably linked to all other patients seeking care; we cannot give to one without taking from another. 'Cost-effectiveness' then becomes a rational standard to guide the shift from all that is possible to all that is affordable. Cost-effectiveness is, then, distinct from cost containment. The latter is managed money while the former is managed care through a rational allocation of resources, presumably physician-guided.

Cost containment, as opposed to cost effectiveness, as a goal may distract and mislead us from our primary physicianly responsibilities. After all, if one considers only the cost to the healthcare system for treatment of a patient from the onset of a specific medical episode, the most cost-saving outcome is an early and sudden death of the patient. At a time when epidemiological data indicate that the vast majority of individuals suffering from such anguishing and impairing disorders as major depression and panic disorders are failing to seek treatment, that only 25% of patients with panic disorder or major depression have actually received treatment at some point, our clinical responsibility is to bring more patients into the healthcare setting where effective treatments are available. A narrow view of healthcare dollar expenditures would see such expansion of health delivery to run counter to the goal of cost containment. How do we set a price on improved diagnosis and increased likelihood of offering treatment even in the absence of identifiable savings? Our clinical mission and cost containment run at cross purposes.

With cost effectiveness as a standard, however, the greater good to society is taken into consideration; when more than cost of a particular intervention is considered but also issues of quality of care, quality of life and cost to society as a whole can the new emphasis on cost effectiveness rest comfortably with the spirit of traditional medicine. This means that cost must be viewed as the total cost and cost offsets to society as a whole for a given treatment. A hospital formulary committee focused only on its own budget may balk at the addition of a new and expensive ulcer drug without recognizing the important cost offset to the system as a whole were this agent to obviate the need for even a few abdominal surgeries. In the case of newer, more costly antidepressant tablets, if a new agent even marginally decreases the risk of hospitalization, the likelihood of falls, serious toxicity or death in overdose, or, over the long term, even the incidence of dental caries, relatively higher tablet costs are quickly offset.

The narrow focus on the cost of a tablet to the formulary may yield more insidious long-term damage in the effort to improve care. The world has generally relied on the use of capital, and in particular the risk of capital, to yield new pharmaceuticals. What impact will the inevitable progress toward price constraint or formulary de-selection of newer agents have on the future of medical development, as capital, adverse to risk without return, moves away from the commercial system of drug development? Physician, inform thyself about the new economics of healthcare.

For the psychiatric clinician, a parallel process necessitating informing those responsible for formulating healthcare policy is also urgently needed. Major depression, by one measure of direct and indirect costs in the US alone (exclusive of quality of life measures) extracts annual costs from society of more than $50 billion (Stoudemire *et al.*, 1986). This disorder also accounts for more people out of work and in bed than other common medical disorders except for significant cardiovascular disorders (Wells *et al.*, 1989) and more net cost to the economy thereby than chronic respiratory illness, diabetes, arthritis or hypertension. Patient suffering, impact on family members, particularly spouses and children, and the substantial lifetime mortality, compel us to diagnose and to make treatment available and tolerable. While major depression is among the most common clinical problems encountered by primary care physicians, the rate of recognition of this illness and the track record of treatment inadequacy— major depression is frequently under-diagnosed and under-treated by the general healthcare system—strongly urge us on to the development of antidepressant interventions that are more user friendly both for the prescriber and the patient. And when the accounting is done as to cost-effectiveness, it must address such issues as the cost of depression to society, the savings to society of decreased worker absenteeism and days lost from work, as well as the cost of treatment failure. In the clinical setting, reality is that the new agents, the SSRIs, are not only better tolerated, and more likely to be effective due to enhanced compliance and decreased premature discontinuation, but when prescribed they will be used in usually adequate doses given their current formulation. Older agents require dose titration as patients accommodate to adverse effects and are rarely administered in therapeutically adequate doses. In clinical trials, where SSRIs are compared to older agents such as the tricyclic antidepressants (TCAs), the research protocols for the depressed patient volunteers (subjects) requires that participants receive at least minimally adequate (or maximally tolerated) treatment. This level of treatment, however, is much less likely to be achieved in the usual primary care clinical setting, thereby obscuring the *efficacy* advantage, and not just the side-effect advantage, of using these newer agents in the naturalistic clinical setting.

Studies suggest that major depression occurs in 5–10% of primary care patients and 10–14% of medical inpatients (Katon and Schulberg, 1992). One report of a community sample of older adults (age 55 and over) indicated that the odds of dying were more than four times greater for individuals with mood disorders than for others in the sample (n=3007) controlled for age, sex, and physical health (Bruce and Leaf, 1989). Lack of treatment and under-treatment in primary care and in older populations is almost certainly partly accountable to the burden of traditional antidepressant treatment: the need for dose titration, uncomfortable side-effects and other risks, and lethality in overdose.

In an important study of 'distressed high utilizers' of primary care, only 11% of patients, deemed by psychiatric evaluation to be in need of antidepressant medication, had received an adequate dosage and duration of pharmacotherapy (Katon *et al.*, 1992). While psychiatric consultation in this primary care setting increased the likelihood of a patient to receive antidepressants, this intervention did not significantly increase the likelihood of the patient to receive adequate antidepressant therapy. However, the likelihood of the patient continuing on the prescribed antidepressant was significantly greater when the initial antidepressant chosen was one with the more favourable side-effect profile, including secondary amine tricyclics (desipramine, nortriptyline) and then 'newer' agents (i.e. trazodone, fluoxetine). The data also indicated that the likelihood of the patient filling a third prescription was 30% if the initial agent was amitriptyline or doxepin as compared with 60% when the initial choice was an SSRI (Katon *et al.*, 1992). Further, only with the SSRI would dosing adequacy have been ensured by the decision to prescribe.

Who will take the broader view with respect to quality of life for the patient, overall cost to the healthcare system, total cost to society, as well as the burdens of pain and suffering experienced not only by the patient but family and friends as well? I suspect not the hospital formulary budget counting the relative cost of tablets for the same diagnostic indication? As stated by Freedman and Stahl (1992), 'Cost containment haunts health policy and has pushed medical practice towards restricted drug formularies and standardized treatment. Such policy attitudes are often inexplicit about the value of innovations needed to cope with inescapable variabilities in drug response'. Forewarned is forearmed and, thus, the rationale for this volume.

Professor Buxton sharply engages and defines the dilemma for us, noting that the 'language of cost-effectiveness' not only pervades the debate about choices but has become the determinant of choice. With the existence or prospect of expensive new technologies, the need to use scarce healthcare resources to maximum benefit is the challenge: (1) costs of what is possible exceed available resources; (2) resources cannot keep up with the cost of marginal improvements; and therefore (3) choices are inevitable. Thus, physicians, trained in a 'clinical decision model' must understand the implications of a 'health economics model'. Can or should the doctor change traditional practice or continue to always do what is determined best for the individual patient and let the payer take the heat? Once aware of the inextricable link between all clinical decisions and scarce healthcare resources, the physician experiences a double-bind, damned if he/she does, damned if he/she doesn't. As noted, a marginal gain for society may involve a life-or-death decision for an individual patient. Urging collaboration between physicians and health economists, Professor Buxton introduced the 'clinical resource management model' with the potential to have physicians responsible for the allocation of resources within the constraints of fixed prospective payments, quality control, and outcome assessment (audit).

Professor Weisbrod starkly serves notice that 'no system can long endure in which one party determines what will be done while another system finances those decisions'. The physician as 'double agent' is left in the middle, required to serve both patient and payer. Professor Weisbrod's important study reminds us to be aware of the costs of reducing costs, that without measuring the costs to society of different treatments or programs we run the risk of simply cost-shifting to other sectors. For example, what may seem like a more costly intervention may be, from a societal point of view, cost-effective when one considers loss in productivity and such other non-healthcare costs as crime and motor vehicle accidents. With respect to cost–benefit analyses of treatment with the mentally ill, acceptability and tolerability of treatment will greatly determine the efficacy and hence the cost-effectiveness of treatment.

Professors Jönsson and Bebbington's simulation model remind us that cost-effectiveness is not congruent with cost of treatment. In examining the cost-effectiveness of a new antidepressant, relying on a top-down study including direct costs only (and not the overall costs of depression), their model underscores the cost of treatment failure as predicted by dropout rates in clinical trial data. In this analysis, the cost per successful treatment favoured the new antidepressant, paroxetine, compared to TCAs. That this finding emerges from clinical trial data is particularly noteworthy when one considers, again, that the difference between older and newer agents will be even more pronounced in naturalistic settings, where a protocol is not driving the prescriber to ensure adequacy, and where under-treatment with older agents is commonplace. However, short-term clinical trials do not measure the importance of treatment effectiveness and tolerability over the long-term. The majority of patients with major depression will have residual symptoms or recurrences and require long-term treatment. For those with a successful acute response to antidepressants, prevention of relapse of a first episode requires 4 or more months of continuation treatment. For a patient with a history of three or more prior episodes, a history of chronic depressive symptoms, or older age of onset of depression, maintenance treatment to prevent recurrence will be measured in years. The long-term data for SSRIs not only attests to their sustained efficacy, but their exceptional tolerability and lack of adverse effects over the long term, in contrast to the persisting adverse effects of tricyclic antidepressants. Thus, the cost-effectiveness of newer agents is likely greater in naturalistic clinical practice where adequate doses as well as compliance with continuation and maintenance therapy are the essence of treatment. Not only are indirect social costs excluded from the Jönsson and Bebbington model, but also such ancillary costs for treatment with older agents as electrocardiograms, plasma levels (particularly in the US where they are considered a standard), costs from toxicity complicating treatment, such as adverse effects from falls, urinary retention, constipation, dental caries and reduced psychomotor performance. No clinician would be surprised to hear that, despite greater cost per tablet, newer agents, even with a conservative economic model, are most cost-effective.

The study by McCombs and Nichol recognizes that the basic elements of adequacy of treatment, dose and duration are extremely rare with the older agents and draws a direct connection between the risk of side-effects and treatment failure. Their analysis, revealing the high cost of treatment failure, is also a conservative estimate, excluding as it does patients who are under-treated, an extremely common circumstance for TCAs prescribed by primary care physicians. The risk of under-treatment and treatment failure is particularly high in the subgroup of elderly depressed patients where sensitivity to side-effects and prescriber concerns about toxicity have traditionally meant inadequate therapy. This finding is replicated by the analyses of Boyer and Feighner evaluating the relationship between treatment dropout, side-effects, treatment failure and hospital cost.

The US is in the midst of designing a new health insurance payment system. A complicated relationship exists between health insurance payment for depression and overall costs as explored in the chapter by Professor McGuire. Health payment systems are importantly linked to outcome by determining access to effective treatment. A health payment system must not only allow access to services with the best outcomes, it must also minimize cost while protecting patients from serious financial risk. These benefits will come from certain trade-offs, particularly limiting hospital costs by decreasing bed days and including cost sharing for the patient.

The Gotland study program described by Professor Wålinder increased the availability and quality of depression treatment by GPs on the island of Gotland. Most participating GPs found the didactic program about depression to be practical and to have increased their competence in handling and treating major depression; referrals to specialists decreased substantially, as did total inpatient days due to depression, sick leave, and the prescribing of sedatives and major tranquilizers. Furthermore, the suicide rate decreased relative to the trends on Gotland and in the rest of Sweden. While the effects of the program were time-limited, the improvement in the quality of care delivered to depressed patients and the savings from the improvement in the treatment of depression were estimated to be over US$26 million, without again considering quality of life issues in the calculation. Indeed, acute, cross-sectional symptom improvement as measured in acute clinical studies may be one window on the therapeutic impact of antidepressant agents, but the essential variable for measuring the clinical effectiveness of treatment is the quality of life for the depressed patient over time. Therefore, treatment studies henceforth would do well to require more than symptom level change measures, and to include quality of life measures. These will also provide a window on indirect costs which will serve to inform the health economic debate on the treatments of major depression. The chapter by Bech *et al.* in this regard is timely and important in setting the standard for this endeavor.

As underscored by Currie and colleagues, quality of life as well as clinical outcome will be enhanced by agents which are safer and more tolerable and therefore more likely to yield an effective clinical outcome: agents which lack overdose toxicity and lethality, agents which lack important behavioral toxicity on measures of psychomotor and cognitive performance and function, agents which lack measurable adverse impact on memory and daytime sedation, and thus lack risks of predisposing to events with substantial costs to society such as fractures from falls and motor vehicles accidents. These risks, typically unmeasured in health economic analyses of treatments, are specifically the reasons why most psychiatrists in the US have turned to the SSRIs as the first line of treatment for major depression, agents which would be selected to treat a family member or a colleague, and thus, agents which represent an advance not only in therapy but also in terms of cost to society, promising increased delivery of adequate treatment of depression by physicians, enhanced compliance by patients overall and, therefore, greater clinical effectiveness of treatment in the short and long term, with resulting improved cost-effectiveness of treatment for society as a whole. With respect to the current intense scrutiny on cost of health care interventions, that there is a narrow focus on formulary costs without consideration of quality of life and total cost to society serves notice to clinicians in general that they must be in a position to inform health policy makers and the general public about the human and societal costs of disorders and the relative acceptability of effective treatments. To this end, health economics serves as an essential tool for this process.

References

Bruce ML and Leaf PJ. Psychiatric disorders and 15 month mortality in a community sample of older adults. *Am J Public Health* **79**, 727–730.

Freedman DX and Stahl SM. Pharmacology: policy implications of new psychiatric drugs. *Health Affairs* **11**, 157–163.

Katon W and Schulberg H. Epidemiology of depression in primary care. *Gen Hosp Psychiatry* **14**, 237–247.

Katon W, Von Korff M, Lin E, Bush T and Ormel J. Adequacy and duration of antidepressant treatment in primary care. *J Med Care* **30**, 67–76.

Stoudemire A, Frank R, Hedemark N, Kamlet M and Blazer D (1986) The economic burden of depression. *Gen Hosp Psychiatry* **8**, 387–394.

Wells KB, Stewart A, Hays RD *et al.* (1989) The functioning and well-being of depressed patients: results from the Medical Outcomes Study. *JAMA* **262**, 914–919.

Index

Note: Page numbers in *italic* refer to figures; those in **bold** refer to tables

Index compiled by Annette Musker